THE
GRAPHIC DESIGN
REFERENCE &
SPECIFICATION
BOOK

Brimming with creative inspiration, how-to projects, and useful information to enrich your everyday life, Quarto Knows is a favorite destination for those pursuing their interests and passions. Visit our site and dig deeper with our books into your area of interest: Quarto Creates, Quarto Cooks, Quarto Homes, Quarto Lives, Quarto Drives, Quarto Explores, Quarto Gifts, or Quarto Kids.

First published in 2013 by Rockport Publishers,
an imprint of The Quarto Group,
100 Cummings Center, Suite 265-D,
Beverly, MA 01915, USA.
T (978) 282-9590 F (978) 283-2742
www.QuartoKnows.com

The Library of Congress has cataloged the earlier edition as follows:
Evans, Poppy
    Forms, folds, and sizes : all the details graphic designers need to know but can neverfind / Poppy Evans.
        p.   cm.
    Includes bibliographical references.
    ISBN 1-59253-054-0 (vinyl)
    1. Printing—Handbooks, manuals, etc. 2. Graphic design (Typography)—Handbooks,
    manuals, etc. 3. Packaging—Handbooks, manuals, etc. 4. Shippers' guides. I. Title.
    Z244.3.E83 2004
    686.2—dc22

                                            2003026487
                                            CIP

ISBN: 978-1-59253-851-5

Digital edition published in 2013
eISBN: 978-1-61-58-788-4

Interior Design: Peter King & Company
Page Layout: Rockport Publishers
Cover Design: Burge Agency, www.burgeacgency.com

Printed in USA

This book was digitally printed, therefore the process color finder, which appeared in the original edition, is not included.

THE GRAPHIC DESIGN REFERENCE & SPECIFICATION BOOK

POPPY EVANS AND AARIS SHERIN
UPDATED MATERIALS PROVIDED BY IRINA LEE

ROCKPORT

Contents

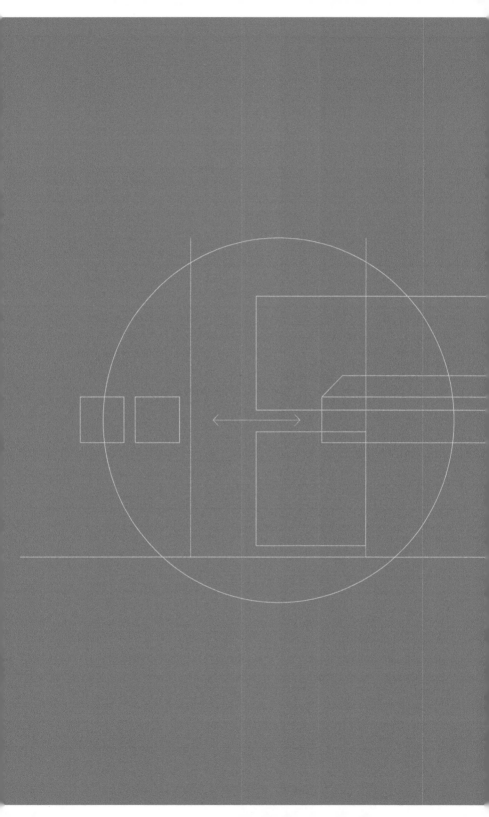

Introduction

Graphic designers and others responsible for preparing printed materials frequently refer to a variety of diagrams, swatches, templates, conversion tables, and other resources that help them do their job. However, few designers have all the resources they need at their fingertips. Those who work independently, or in small studio environments, often find themselves wasting time searching the Web or seeking out other sources for the information they need. Others in large studio or agency environments may have access to a vast library of resources but find themselves spending just as much time looking through volumes of materials before they find the information they need.

The Graphic Design Reference and Specification Book is a compilation of essential information—a reference manual that provides designers with information they need on a daily basis, from consulting a library of type samples, to identifying a specific font, to checking the style and dimensions of a specific type of envelope, to under-standing when it is appropriate to abbreviate a state or country name in the acceptable format. There's even a bibliography at the end of the book to help, if additional information is needed.

The Graphic Design Reference and Specification Book was created to answer the questions that designers ask most often and to deliver this information in a concise, understandable, and easy-to-access way. No frills, no excess—just bottom-line information to help you produce your projects.

Chapter 1: Measurement Conversion Charts

MILLIMETERS, POINTS, AND PICAS TO INCHES

mm	points	picas	inches
1.586	4.513	0.375	$\frac{1}{16}$
3.175	9.034	0.75	$\frac{1}{8}$
4.763	13.552	1.125	$\frac{3}{16}$
6.35	18.068	1.5	$\frac{1}{4}$
7.938	22.586	1.875	$\frac{5}{16}$
9.525	27.101	2.25	$\frac{3}{8}$
11.113	31.620	2.635	$\frac{7}{16}$
12.7	36.135	3.011	$\frac{1}{2}$
14.288	40.653	3.388	$\frac{9}{16}$
15.875	45.169	3.764	$\frac{5}{8}$
17.463	49.687	4.140	$\frac{11}{16}$
19.050	54.203	4.517	$\frac{3}{4}$
21.638	61.566	5.130	$\frac{13}{16}$
22.225	63.236	5.270	$\frac{7}{8}$
23.813	67.755	5.646	$\frac{15}{16}$
25.4	72.27	6.022	1 inch

INCH DECIMALS TO INCH FRACTIONS

decimals	fractions	decimals	fractions
0.063	$1/16$	0.531	$17/32$
0.094	$3/32$	0.563	$9/16$
0.125	$1/8$	0.594	$19/32$
0.156	$5/32$	0.625	$5/8$
0.188	$3/16$	0.656	$21/32$
0.219	$7/32$	0.688	$11/16$
0.250	$1/4$	0.719	$21/32$
0.281	$9/32$	0.75	$3/4$
0.313	$5/16$	0.781	$25/32$
0.344	$11/32$	0.813	$13/16$
0.375	$3/8$	0.844	$27/32$
0.406	$13/32$	0.875	$7/8$
0.438	$7/16$	0.906	$29/32$
0.469	$15/32$	0.938	$15/16$
0.5	$1/2$	0.969	$31/32$
		1.000	1 inch

CONVERSION FORMULAS

1 inch	2.54 centimeters
	25.4 millimeters
	72.27 points
	6.0225 picas
1 foot	30.5 centimeters
1 yard	0.9 meter
1 meter	1.1 yards
1 centimeter	0.03 foot
	0.4 inch
1 millimeter	0.0394 inch
	2.8453 points
	0.2371 pica
1 point	0.0138 inch
	0.08335 pica
	0.3515 millimeter
1 pica	0.166 inch
	4.2175 millimeters
	12 points

1 square (sq.) inch	6.45 sq. centimeters
1 sq. centimeter	0.16 sq. inch
1 sq. foot	0.09 sq. meter
1 sq. meter	10.8 sq. feet
1 sq. yard	0.8 sq. meter
1 sq. meter	1.2 sq. yards
1 pound	0.45 kilogram
1 kilogram	2.2 pounds
1 ounce	28.4 grams
1 gram	0.04 ounce

METRIC TO IMPERIAL EQUIVALENTS

25.4 millimeters	1 inch
304.8 millimeters	1 foot
914.4 millimeters	1 yard

○ Chapter 2: Copyright and Trademark Standards

COPYRIGHT

Copyright is defined as the exclusive legal right to reproduce, publish, and sell a literary, musical, or artistic work. Anything that is produced is a copyrighted piece of work as soon as it is produced if it falls under one of the above categories. In the United States, a work is under the protection of copyright from the moment it is created until seventy years after its author's death. During that period, the owner of a copyrighted work owns the rights to its reproduction, display, distribution, and adaptation to derivative works. (Note that a "work" can be copyrighted, but not an idea. Ideas must be patented.) A *copyright infringement* occurs when somebody copies a copyright protected work owned by someone else or exercises an exclusive right without authorization.

A *copyright notice*, strategically placed on literary, musical, or artistic work, serves as a warning to potential plagiarizers. A copyright notice consists of the word "Copyright" or its symbol, ©, the year the work was created or first published, and the full name of the copyright owner. Example: © 2013 John Doe. For HTML pages, use the HTML number code **©** to insert a copyright notice. Example: <p>© 2013 John Doe</p>.

The copyright notice should be placed where it can be easily seen. Placing a copyright notice on a piece of work isn't absolutely necessary to claim copyright infringement, but it is in the owner's best interest to use this symbol as a warning. Original work can be further protected by registering it with the U.S. Copyright Office:

U.S. Copyright Office
101 Independence Ave. S.E.
Washington, D.C. 20559-6000
(202) 707-3000 or 1-877-476-0778 (toll free)
www.copyright.gov

Registering an artistic work requires filing an application with the Copyright Office and accompanying it with two visual representations, in printed for digital form, of the work being registered. There is a $65 (£40) nonrefundable fee for paper registration and a $35 (£21) non-refundable fee for electronic filing. Application forms can be found online at *www.copyright.gov/forms*. The work becomes registered on the date that all the required elements for registration are received by the U.S. Copyright Office.

PUBLIC DOMAIN

Older artistic creations, which are no longer protected by copyright, fall into a category called "public domain," and can be used by anyone without obtaining permission or paying a fee. Uncredited or anonymous works are no longer protected by copyright beyond 95 years after the date of their publication or 120 years after their creation. Works credited to an artist or author are no longer protected beyond 70 years after the creator's death.

TRANSFERRING RIGHTS

Transferring a copyright means granting permission to another to use or publish the work on a temporary basis. Some common types of transfer rights include the following:

First rights: The work is leased for one use where it is published for the first time.

One-time rights: The work is leased for one use, but there is no guarantee that the buyer is the first to have published the work.

Exclusive rights: The leaser retains the right to use or publish the work exclusively in their industry. With an arrangement of this type, an artistic work that appears in a magazine may not appear in another magazine, however it could be used on a greeting card.

Reprint rights: The leaser is given the right to use or publish the work after it has appeared elsewhere. Also called serial rights.

Promotion rights: The leaser is given the right to use the work for promotional purposes. This type of agreement is often tacked onto another rights contract. For instance, an agreement with a greeting card company to use an illustration on a greeting card would include a promotion rights clause giving the company the right to use the same illustration in its promotion of the card.

CREATIVE COMMONS LISCENSING

Creative Commons is a non-profit organization that provides free copyright licenses to help creative professionals give others the ability to share, use, or build upon the worked they have created. A Creative Commons license gives designers the flexibility to share their work without relegating it to the public domain. The standardized Creative Commons license allows designers to set up copyright terms based on the conditions of their choice.

What can Creative Commons do for designers?
Designers can use Creative Commons to set up legal notices that permit others to use their content. For example, a designer can use Creative Commons license to set specific conditions for use for an infographic designed as a personal project. By using a Creative Commons license, any person, or organization, can use that specifc infographic, without permission, as long as the infographic is used in a manner that meets the conditions the designer outlined in the license.

Creative Commons License Types:
There are six major Creative Commons licenses that can be used when publishing work. At a minimum each license retains copyright, attributes authorship, applies worldwide and lasts for the duration of the works copyright.

Attribution (CC-BY)
The most accommodating license type, the Attribution license allows others to distribute, edit, and improve a designer's original work, even for commercial reasons, as long as the original designer is credited for the original work.

Attribution Share Alike (BY-SA):
The Attribution Share Alike license type allows others to edit and improve upon a designer's work, even for commercial reasons, as long as the original designer is given credit, and the new creation is licensed under the same terms.

Attribution No Derivatives (BY-ND)
The Attribution No Derivatives license allows commercial and non-commercial redistribution as long as the original designer is given credit, and no changes are made to the original work.

Attribution Non-Commercial (CC-BY-NC)
The Attribution Non-Commercial license allows others to edit and improve upon a designer's work non-commercially as long as the original designer is given credit. However, any new work created from the designer's original work will not be licensed under the same terms.

Attribution Non-Commercial Share Alike
The Attribution Non-Commercial Share Alike license allows others to edit and improve upon a designer's work non-commercially as long as the original designer is given credit and any new work created from the original is licensed under the same terms. Any new work created form the original must also be non-commercial in use.

Attribution Non-Commercial No Derivatives
The most restrictive of the Creative Commons licenses, Attribution Non-Commercial No Derivatives allows others to non-commercially redistribute a designer's original work. It is often referred to as "free-advertising" because it allows others to distribute a designer's work as long as the designer is credited and the work is unchanged.

TRADEMARKS AND SERVICE MARKS

A trademark is a word(s), phrase(s), symbol(s), or design(s) that distinguishes the source of a product from one originator from those of another. A service mark is the same as a trademark except that it distinguishes the source of a service. An infringement occurs when somebody uses or mimics an existing trademark or service mark to represent another product or service so that others are misled into believing they are purchasing the original product or service. It is not necessary to register a logo or mark. A user can establish rights with a mark based on its legitimate use. However, owning a federal trademark registration has advantages:

1. Providing legal presumption of the registrant's ownership of the mark and exclusive right to use the mark and the ability to bring legal action concerning misuse of the mark.

2. The right to obtain registration in foreign countries and ability to file the U.S. registration with the U.S. Customs Service to prevent importation of infringing foreign goods.

3. Ability to display notice to the public of claim of ownership through the use of the ® symbol.

Users can use the symbols ™ (trademark) and ᔞᴹ (service mark) to alert the public to their claim of rights to a mark, regardless of whether an application has been filed with the United States Patent and Trademark Office (USPTO). However, the federal registration symbol ® can only be used after the USPTO actually registers a mark and not while an application is pending. The registration symbol can only be used with the mark on, or in connection with, the goods and/or services listed in the federal trademark registration.

Registering a trademark or service mark requires filing an application with the United States Patent and Trademark Office.

USPTO at Commissioner for Trademarks
2900 Crystal Drive
Arlington, VA 22202-3514
(703) 308-9000 (Trademark Assistance Center)
uspto.gov/trademarks/teas/index.jsp

LEGAL RESOURCES

Although not required, using a private trademark attorney for legal advice in filing an application may help you avoid many potential pitfalls. Additionally, several free legal resources may be helpful in the process. You may also consult free legal resources pertaining to your specific state of residence.

List of free legal resources
Nolo (nolo.com)
Online library of do-it-yourself legal books and software for simple legal matters.

Voluteer Lawyers for the Arts (vlany.org)
A New York–based organization that offers volunteer legal services to arts organizations and individual artists nationwide.

Chapter 3: Proofreading and Copywriting

PROOFREADERS' SYMBOLS

These marks and notations are widely used and understood by editors, proofreaders, and others involved in writing and producing text. Use them when proofing or editing a manuscript or proof.

Explanation	Mark	How Used
Delete or take out	ℒ	Treasure Island, by Robert Lewiss Stevenson ℒ
Insert	∧	Treasure Island, Robert Lewis Stevenson by∧
Let it stand	stet	Treasure Island, By Robert Lewis Stevenson stet
Close up	◯	Treasure Island, by Robert Lewis S tevenson
Spell out	SP	Treasure Island, by Robt Lewis Stevenson SP
Boldface	bf	Treasure Island, by Robert Lewis Stevenson bf
Italics	ital	Treasure Island, by Robert Lewis Stevenson ital
Roman	rom	Treasure Island by Robert Lewis Stevenson rom
Correct alignment	=	Treasure Island, by Robert Lewis Stevenson align
Transpose these items	∼	Island Treasure by Robert Lewis Stevenson ∼
Wrong font	wf	Treasure Island, by Robert Lewis Stevenson wf
Lowercase	/ lc	TReAsUrE Island, by Robert Lewis Stevenson lc
Uppercase	≡ uc	treasure Island, by Robert Lewis Stevenson uc
Space	#	Treasure Island, by Robert LewisStevenson #
Period	⊙	
Ellipsis or leader dots	⋯	
Begin new paragraph	¶	
Em dash	em	
En dash	en	
Move right	⊐	
Move left	⊏	

FOOTNOTES

Notes and footnotes always end with periods, even if they do not form complete sentences. Source lines do not end in periods. Use the following sequence when listing more than one footnote per page:

*   First footnote
†   Second footnote
**   Third footnote
‡   Fourth footnote

ABBREVIATION GUIDE

When to abbreviate a word or name and how to abbreviate it will vary, depending on how it is used. Consult the following categories for usage advice on any given term or name and its abbreviation.

Time Designations

When designating an hour of the day, use figures for clock time followed by a.m. and p.m. Midnight, noon, 12:00 midnight, or 12:00 noon are preferred to 12:00 p.m. or 12:00 a.m. Use AD preceding the year, with no comma (AD 2004); BC following the year, with no comma (115 BC). Use abbreviations for seconds, minutes, hours, weeks, and months in tables and charts only. Spell out in all other situations.

Meaning	Abbreviation	Meaning	Abbreviation
after the birth of Christ	AD or A.D.	January	Jan.
before the birth of Christ	BC or B.C.	February	Feb.
before noon	a.m.	March	Mar.
after noon	p.m.	April	Apr.
century	cent.	May	May
year	yr.	June	June
month	mo.	July	July
months	mos.	August	Aug.
week	wk.	September	Sep.
hour	hr.	October	Oct.
minute	min.	November	Nov.
seconds	sec.	December	Dec.
Monday	Mon.		
Tuesday	Tues.		
Wednesday	Wed.		
Thursday	Thur.		
Friday	Fri.		
Saturday	Sat.		
Sunday	Sun.		

United States State Abbreviations

When the name of a U.S. state appears as part of a complete mailing address, use the postal service abbreviation.

State	Postal Service Abbreviation	State	Postal Service Abbreviation
Alabama	AL	Montana	MT
Alaska	AK	Nebraska	NE
Arizona	AZ	Nevada	NV
Arkansas	AR	New Hampshire	NH
California	CA	New Jersey	NJ
Colorado	CO	New Mexico	NM
Connecticut	CT	New York	NY
Delaware	DE	North Carolina	NC
District of Columbia	DC	North Dakota	ND
Florida	FL	Ohio	OH
Georgia	GA	Oklahoma	OK
Hawaii	HI	Oregon	OR
Idaho	ID	Pennsylvania	PA
Illinois	IL	Rhode Island	RI
Indiana	IN	South Carolina	SC
Iowa	IA	South Dakota	SD
Kansas	KS	Tennessee	TN
Kentucky	KY	Texas	TX
Louisiana	LA	Utah	UT
Maine	ME	Vermont	VT
Maryland	MD	Virginia	VA
Massachusetts	MA	Washington	WA
Michigan	MI	West Virginia	WV
Minnesota	MN	Wisconsin	WI
Mississippi	MS	Wyoming	WY
Missouri	MO		

United States Territories

Territory	Postal Service Abbreviation
American Samoa	AS
Federated States of Micronesia	FM
Guam	GU
Marshall Islands	MH
Palau	PW
Puerto Rico	PR
Virgin Islands	VI

Weights and Measures

UNITED STATES		INTERNATIONAL	
mile	mi.	kilometer	km
yard(s)	yd.	meter	m
foot	ft.	centimeter	cm
inch	in.	millimeter	mm
ton(s)	t.	metric ton	t
pounds	lb.	kilogram	kg
ounces	oz.	gram	g
pint	pt.	liter	L
quart	qt.	milliliter	mL
gallon	gal.	British thermal unit	Btu
horsepower	hp.	calorie	cal.
miles per gallon	mpg	hectare	ha
miles per hour	mph	hertz	Hz

Common Prefixes

Prefix	Symbol	Factor
mega-		M
1,000,000		
kilo-		k
1,000		
centi-		c
1/100		
milli-		m
1/1,000		

NUMBER AND NUMERAL USAGE

Check the following guidelines for when to use numerals or spell out numbers and dates:

· In general, spell out cardinal and ordinal numbers below 10 (four days). Use figures for numbers 10 and up (15 people) unless they begin a sentence (fifteen people entered the house).

· Weights, measures, figure numbers, times, and dates should always be stated numerically.

· Numbers that would normally be spelled out might get confusing in sequence. Switch to numerals when stating more than one numerical description in sequence (he filled 12 eight-oz. glasses).

· Add an s to numerals and dates to pluralize them (1950s, '70s, B-52s).

HYPHENATION GUIDE

There are differences in length between the hyphen (-), the en dash (–) and the em dash (—). An en dash is roughly the width of an n; an em dash is the width of an m. Each has its proper place in written language.

Hyphen: Use in words that are broken over two lines (*pro-ject*), fractions (*a two-thirds majority*), multiple modifiers (part-time employee) or in a compound adjective, verb, or adverb (*Italian-American*).

En dash: Use to indicate ranges in a numerical sequence (*January 23–25, 2001; pages 53–66; 1–2 tbsp of sugar*), in other designations of time (*May–June*), or when combining open compounds (*Maryland–Virginia border*).

Em dash: Use as punctuation in place of a semicolon or a colon (*The computer industry was in full bloom—many technological methods were well established*), or to indicate a pause of thought, or to precede a quote attribution (*"Never mistake motion for action."—Ernest Hemingway*).

PRIME MARKS AND QUOTATION MARKS GUIDE

Prime marks: Use to indicate inches (8" deep dish pizza) and feet (*He is 6'2" with green eyes.*) Never use in place of quotation marks or apostrophes.

Quotation marks: Use to indicate opening and closing of a quote (*"This is a proper use of quotation marks," she said.*) Use single close quote mark as apostrophes for contractions or possessions (*That's Ethan's toy.*)

Hanging punctuation: also known as **extendation**, is the proper way to treat quotation marks and bullet points to keep a clean margin of alignment.

"Lorem ipsum dolor sit amet,
consectetur adipisicing elit,
sed do eiusmod tempor incididunt
ut labore et dolore magna aliqua."

   Lorem ipsum dolor sit amet,
consectetur adipisicing elit
   Sed do eiusmod tempor
incididunt ut labore et dolore
magna aliqua.

Improper typesetting of quotation marks and bullet points where the punctuation disrupt the body of text and break the margin of alignment.

"Lorem ipsum dolor sit amet,
consectetur adipisicing elit,
sed do eiusmod tempor incididunt
ut labore et dolore magna aliqua."

Lorem ipsum dolor sit amet,
consectetur adipisicing elit
Sed do eiusmod tempor
incididunt ut labore et dolore
magna aliqua.

Hanging punctuation pushes the quotation marks and bullet points into the margin, thus creating a clean paragraph of text.

○ Chapter 4: Imaging and Color

UNDERSTANDING IMAGE FILE FORMATS

Digital files can be saved in a number of file formats. For any type of file, the extension at the end (for example, "JohnDoePortrait.raw") indicates the format in which your file has been saved. Each file format has a purpose. Refer to the chart below for saving and working with files—whether you want to use the files for editing, posting online, sharing via email or printing.

Format	Definition	Advantage	Disadvantage
EPS or .eps	Used for placing images or graphics in documents created in word processing, page layout, or drawing programs. Supports both rastered and vectored data. EPS files can be cross-platformed, cropped, or edited.		
GIF or .gif (Graphics Interchange Format)	An 8-bit, low-memory option for posting images online. GIF images are limited to 256 colors, making them unsuitable for most print applications. Ideally suited for the limited color display range of computer monitors. GIFs are well-suited for images containing large, flat areas of one color and are often used for graphics such as logos and line art. Commonly used for Web graphics with a limited color range rather than photographs.	Because they use fewer colors, GIF file sizes are very small, which makes them perfect for online use.	GIF files don't support as many colors as other types of file formats.
JPEG or .jpg (Joint Photographic Experts Group)	File format designated by the Joint Photographic Experts Group for image compression. Because it is a "lossy" compression format, image quality is sacrificed to conserve disk space. JPEGs are frequently used for placing imagery in websites and online applications where high resolution files aren't necessary. JPEGs work best for photographs, illustrations, and other complex imagery.	JPEG has the highest compression and therefore offers the smallest file size. It is also the most common file format and is supported by almost every photo-editing or photo-organization program.	Unlike RAW and TIFF formats, a JPEG will degrade each time it is saved. This is known as a "lossy" type of compression.

Format	Definition	Advantage	Disadvantage
PDF or .pdf (Portable Document Format)	Used for allowing documents to be viewed and printed independent of the application used to create them. Often used for transferring printed pages over the Web, either for downloading existing publications or for sending documents to commercial printers for output. Commonly used sharing through e-mail and over the Internet.		
TIFF or .tif (Tagged Image File Format)	Used for placing images or graphics in documents created in word processing, page layout, or drawing programs. Supports rasterized data and converts vectored images to bits. TIFF files can be cropped or edited. Similar to EPS, but smaller file size saves memory over EPS format.	TIFF supports layered files, which allows editing images in software programs like Photoshop. TIFFs retain color information while being much smaller than RAW. Can be saved with minimum compression making it ideal for printing large sized high-resolution images.	Though smaller than RAW files, TIFF files are not small. Depending on the resolution of your camera, files can be in the 5 to 15MB range. TIFFs are not widely supported by Web browsers, which makes them a poor choice for online use.
RAW (Extension varies per camera brand. For example, .nef for Nikon, .cr2 for Canon)	Professional-grade cameras offer a couple more compression formats, like RAW. The RAW file format is best for archiving because it is the purest unaltered format available (retains the most digital information). Sometimes referred to as a digital negative.	No compression has been applied. Every bit of information collected from a camera's sensor has been preserved.	RAW image files can be very large, upwards of 40 to 50MB per photo with a high-megapixel camera. Once a RAW image has been manipulated, a copy has to be saved in another form, such as a TIFF or JPEG.

HALFTONE SCREENS

The halftone screens that are used to convert a continuous-tone image to one that can be printed come in a variety of densities measured by lines per inch (lpi), a term the industry uses for referring to the size of a screen's halftone dot. High screen rulings of 175 or 200 lpi have more halftone dots per inch and, therefore, smaller dots. Low screen rulings such as 65 or 85 lpi have larger dots. The size of a halftone dot can affect an image's quality. Those with a high lpi show more detail. However, the choice of halftone screen is often dictated by the type of paper used. Paper with a low degree of absorbency, such as coated stocks, tend to resist dot gain or the spreading of halftone dots in a halftone screen and are suitable for high lpi halftone screens. Printing images on inexpensive uncoated stocks, such as newsprint, tends to result in dot gain and requires a halftone screen with a low lpi.

Enlarged halftone screen.

Shown are some common halftone screens as applied to the same photograph.

65 lpi screen.

100 lpi screen.

150 lpi screen.

200 lpi screen.

TINT VALUES FOR HALFTONE SCREENS

Screen rulings affect the perception of a screen tint as well as how overprints and reverses are perceived against the tints. Consult the chart to the right to get an idea of how a reverse or overprint will look against a screened background.

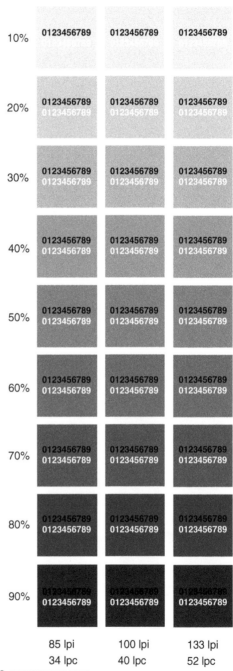

	85 lpi 34 lpc	100 lpi 40 lpc	133 lpi 52 lpc
10%	0123456789	0123456789	0123456789
20%	0123456789	0123456789	0123456789
30%	0123456789	0123456789	0123456789
40%	0123456789	0123456789	0123456789
50%	0123456789	0123456789	0123456789
60%	0123456789	0123456789	0123456789
70%	0123456789	0123456789	0123456789
80%	0123456789	0123456789	0123456789
90%	0123456789	0123456789	0123456789

DUOTONES

A duotone is a halftone printed in two colors, usually black and a second color. One plate is made for the black, picking up the highlights and shadow areas; a second plate is made for the second color, picking up the middle tones. When combined, the two plates produce a monochromatic reproduction with a full range of tones.

Red impression

Black impression

Duotone printed in red and black

FINDING THE BEST SCANNING RESOLUTION

When you select a dpi for an image scan, you are designating the amount of image information your scanner will capture—the higher the dpi, the more image data, or potential for clarity your image file will have. Although scanning at a high dpi may ensure that every detail of your image will be captured, the large size of high-resolution image files makes them cumbersome to work with. Scanning at optimum resolution means getting the best image clarity and reproduction you can achieve with the lowest possible file size or dpi.

To choose the best scanning resolution for an image, start with your image output in mind:

- *Digital display*—Anything that will be displayed on a computer monitor or as part of a digital presentation (PowerPoint, etc) should be scanned at 72 dpi. This is the best image reproduction you can achieve, because a computer monitor's resolution is just 72 dpi. .

- *Print output for studio printers*— Scanning for print reproduction depends on your output device. A 300 dpi studio printer requires images scanned at 300 dpi for optimum clarity. Let this 300 dpi rule of thumb be your guide when scanning line art and continuous-tone imagery for studio output.

- *Print output for commercial printers*— The scanning resolution for a continuous tone image such as photograph or illustration that will be converted to a halftone should be dictated by the lpi of your halftone screen. When scanning for halftone output, the scanning resolution for your image should be a dpi that is double the lpi of your line screen. For example, a photograph reproduced with a 150 lpi halftone screen (standard for a magazine) should be scanned at 300 dpi. However, if the same photograph appears in a newspaper (where halftone screens are generally 85 lpi), the scanning dpi should be 170 dpi.

SCALING AN IMAGE

Beyond output, the other consideration to keep in mind when scanning an image is scale. Reflective art that is reduced will gain clarity, whereas, reflective art that is enlarged will lose it. For instance, when a 300 dpi scanned image is enlarged by 200 percent double its original size), its image resolution is reduced to 150 dpi. If the same image is reduced by 50 percent, its resolution becomes 600 dpi. It's best to scale your image to a size that is close to the size it will appear in its final destination, and then pick the appropriate dpi.

When scaling an image, use this formula to arrive at the right percentage:

Size of your reduction or enlargement × 100 ÷ the size of your original = percentage.

Example: 8″ image scaled to 4″ (4 × 100 = 400 ÷ 8 = 50%)

STANDARD DIGITAL IMAGE SIZES FOR WEB

When considering images for online use, note that there are many variations. However, there are several common standards. For example, if you make your images larger than 460 pixels, most standard blogs will not be able to fit this size into a standard post. Below are several standard image sizes:

· **Thumbnail:** 150px in the long dimension, or smaller, for example 75 × 75px

· **Small:** 240px in the long dimension

· **Medium:** 460px in the long dimension

· **Large:** 520px in the long dimension

· **Very large:** 800px in the long dimension

Common best practices for using images around the Web: use a thumbnail linked to a larger version; decrease the image resolution to 72dpi; use JPEG format for photos and GIF format for text or line art.

STANDARD AD UNIT GUIDELINES

To prepare images for use in advertising units, consult the **Ad Unit Guidelines** developed by the IAB for standard sizes for banners, skyscrapers and buttons in various sizes. Advertising units come in three categories: **Skyscrapers and verticals; horizontals and buttons; rectangles and squares.**

Interactive Advertising Bureau (IAB)
116 East 27th Street, 7th Floor
New York, New York 10016
(212) 380-4700
www.iab.net

○ Chapter 5: Type

TYPE BASICS AND TERMINOLOGY

Because type is measured and described in a language that is unique to the printed word, it is important to recognize and understand basic typographic terms.

Typeface: The design of a single set of letterforms, numerals, and punctuation marks unified by consistent visual properties. Typeface designs are identified by name, such as Arial or Palantino.

Type style: Modifications in a typeface that create design variety while maintaining the visual character of the typeface. These include variations in weight (light, medium, book, bold, heavy, and black), width (condensed or extended) or angle (italic or oblique vs. roman or upright).

Type family: A range of style variations based on a single typeface. Style attributes of type families can contain a number of modifications but will always retain a distinct visual continuity.

Type font: A complete set of letterforms (uppercase and lowercase), numerals, and punctuation marks in a particular typeface that allows for typesetting by keystroke on a computer or other means of typographic composition.

Letterform: The particular style and form of each individual letter in an alphabet.

Character: Individual letterforms, numerals, punctuation marks, or other units that are part of a font.

Uppercase: The capital or larger letters of a type font (A, B, C, etc).

Lowercase: Smaller letters, as opposed to capital letters (a, b, c, etc.).

Univers 55

Univers Bold Extended

Univers Extra Black

Univers Ultra Condensed

Univers Thin Ultra Condensed

The type family of Univers is composed of style variations on the Univers design that include a variety of weights.

CATEGORIZING TYPEFACES

There are many ways of classifying typefaces, however, one of the most obvious is to separate typefaces into one of two categories based on their legibility. Because those who manufacture and work with type make this distinction, typefaces are generally broken down into text and display classifications.

Cap height — Uppercase letter — Ascender — x height — Serif — Baseline — Lowercase letter — Bowl — Loop — Counter — Descender

A knowledge of letterform anatomy is essential to understanding how typefaces differ and distinguishing one typeface from another.

Text typefaces are highly legible and used mostly for large areas of text.

Times
Arial
Garamond

Text typefaces such as Times, Arial, and Garamond have a more traditional look and are easy on the eye. They work well for long passages of text.

Display typefaces are more decorative and not as legible. They tend to catch attention and/or convey a mood or attitude. They are mostly used for single or grouped words such as logotypes, headlines, or phrases.

Impact

Old English

Suburban

Display typefaces such as Impact, Old English, and Suburban are more expressive than text typefaces but are not suitable for large bodies of text.

SERIF AND SANS SERIF

Graphic arts professionals have devised other ways of organizing typefaces. A major distinction is the difference between serif and sans serif typefaces.

Serif

Serif typefaces originated with the Romans who identified their stone shrines and public buildings with chisel-cut letterforms. To hide the ragged ends of these letterforms, the Romans would cut a short, extra stroke on the ends of their letters. This extra cut was called a serif.

Sans serif

Sans serif typefaces were born out of the Industrial Revolution to reflect a more modern aesthetic. They are characterized by no serifs and a smooth, streamlined look.

Serif typefaces can be further broken down into subcategories that make distinctions between the types of serifs they display and their letter stroke style.

Old Style Roman typefaces are styled after classic Roman inscriptions. They have splayed stems, wedge-shaped serifs, and bracketed serifs.

Modern Roman typefaces show an extreme contrast between thick and thin strokes, with sharp, thin serifs.

Transitional Roman typefaces fall in between Old Style and Modern serif typefaces and exhibit characteristics of both.

Egyptian or Slab Serif typefaces have square serifs and even strokes with no thick and thin contrast. (Alternative term: Square Serif.)

Typefaces that resemble handwriting or hand lettering fall into a category called script. All other typefaces fall into a category called decorative. These typefaces are highly stylized and suitable only for display purposes.

PAINTED

Calligraphy

The script category of typefaces includes a variety of looks ranging from typefaces that resemble crude brush-painted signage to those that mimic the calligraphic look of pen and ink.

Modula

Sand

Decorative typefaces, such as the ones shown here, include period and novelty looks. They are most often used to attract attention and convey a mood.

MEASURING TYPE

Type is measured by points, a unit for measuring the height of type and vertical distance between lines of type. A point measures .0138 of an inch or 3.515 mm. There are 72.27 points in an inch and 28.453 points in a millimeter.

8 point

10 point

18 point

24 point

36 point

48 point

60 point

72 point

The point system of measuring type goes back to the days of metal type when sizes were classified according to the metal slug that held each character.

The amount of space between lines of type, called leading, is also measured in points. The term is derived from metal type where strips of lead were inserted between lines of type. (Alternative terms: line spacing, interline spacing.)

Type size:
14 points ⌈ Type can be timeless or trendy.

It can express a mood or an attitude.

Leading:
17 points ⌊ It can function as shape or line in a

composition, or as a pattern or texture.

Line length: 22 picas

Leading is typically one to two points more than the point size of a typeface. This allowance between lines provides enough space to accommodate the height of uppercase characters and ascenders as well as characters with descenders that fall below the baseline.

The horizontal length of a line of type, or its line length, is traditionally measured in picas, but can also be measured in inches or millimeters. There are 6.0230 picas in 1 inch and 2.371 millimeters in a pica.

The distance between characters in a word or number and between words and punctuation in a line of type is called letterspacing. (Alternative terms: tracking or kerning.)

LETTER

LETTER

Adding letterspacing to a word gives it a different aesthetic that may add design value in single or limited word applications. However, lack of legibility makes this technique inappropriate for lengthy amounts of text.

This guide includes alphabetical listings of typefaces and specimens. It is divided into two sections. The first section is limited to single-word representations, by name of display typefaces. The typefaces are organized according to whether they are decorative, scripts, or period looks. The text typeface section includes alphabets and numbers for many of the style variations that are available for each typeface.

Note: This guide is intended as a reference source and not as a font catalog. Check with your font supplier for additional information on style variations and font availability.

Type Specimens: Display Typefaces
Use this guide to identify typefaces that you're trying to match or when considering typefaces for possible use.

Decorative

Aachen
Alternate Gothic
Americana
Aquarius
Balloon
City
Dom Casual
Friz Quadrata
Hobo
Impact
MACHINE
Modula
Octopus
Old English Text
Peignot
Russell Square
Sand
STENCIL
Suburban
Tekton
University
Windsor

Scripts

Brush
Commercial Script
Gillies Gothic Bold
Mistral
Murray Hill
Park Avenue
Zapf Chancery

Period Looks

Bauhaus
Broadway
BUSORAMA
Davida
Playbill
Premier

The stylistic characteristics of decorative and display fonts make it relatively easy to differentiate between these typefaces. However, identifying typefaces within the text category can be more difficult. Looking for subtle differences is often the only way of differentiating one typeface from the next. Here are some guidelines to follow when trying to identify a typeface.

At first glance, these typefaces seem as though they could be the same font, particularly if you compare the uppercase "A's" on the samples set in Arial and Avant Garde. However, there are subtle differences:

· Looking at the x-height of a typeface can often help to identify it. The x-height of the letters in the Futura sample is smaller than those in the Arial and Avant Garde samples.

· The lowercase "a" can differ from one typeface to the next, as it does when comparing the sample set in Arial to those set in Avant Garde and Futura. When trying to identify a typeface, looking at the lowercase "a" will often help determine if there is a match.

Like the sans serif examples here, these serif typefaces all appear similar when you compare the uppercase "A's." The differences in these fonts can be discerned by making some comparisons.

· The x-height of the letters in the Times New Roman sample is smaller than those in the Palatino and Georgia samples.

· When comparing serif typefaces, comparing the style of the serifs can help identify a font. The Palatino and Times New Roman samples have bracketed serifs, whereas the Georgia sample does not. Bracketed serifs are slightly flared out where they join the letter.

· Comparing lowercase letterforms, especially "g's" and "f's," is a good way to note subtle differences. Notice how the loop on the "g's" descender differs between typefaces as well as the form of the letter "f."

Arial
A Hamburger fonts

Avant Garde
A Hamburger fonts

Futura
A Hamburger fonts

Palatino
A Hamburger fonts

Georgia
A Hamburger fonts

Times New Roman
A Hamburger fonts

The typefaces in this section include many of the style variations that are part of each typeface family. However, due to space limitations, condensed, extended, italic, and oblique versions have been limited to the Roman, book, or medium weight of each typeface. Condensed and extended versions of each typeface have also been restricted to one sample.

American Typewriter
ABCDEFGHIJKLMNOPQRSTUVWXYZabcdefghijklmnopq
rstuvwxyz1234567890

American Typewriter Light
ABCDEFGHIJKLMNOPQRSTUVWXYZabcdefghijklmnopqr
stuvwxyz1234567890

American Typewriter Bold
**ABCDEFGHIJKLMNOPQRSTUVWXYZabcdefghijklmno
pqrstuvwxyz1234567890**

American Typewriter Condensed
ABCDEFGHIJKLMNOPQRSTUVWXYZabcdefghijklmnopqrstuvwxyz
1234567890

Americana
ABCDEFGHIJKLMNOPQRSTUVWXYZabcdefghijklmnop
qrstuvwxyz1234567890

Americana Italic
*ABCDEFGHIJKLMNOPQRSTUVWXYZabcdefghijklmnopq
rstuvwxyz1234567890*

Americana Bold
ABCDEFGHIJKLMNOPQRSTUVWXYZabcdefghijklmnop
qrstuvwxyz1234567890

Avenir Light
ABCDEFGHIJKLMNOPQRSTUVWXYZabcdefghijklmnopqrstuvw
xyz1234567890

Avenir Regular
ABCDEFGHIJKLMNOPQRSTUVWXYZabcdefghijklmnopqrstuv
wxyz1234567890

Avenir Regular Oblique

ABCDEFGHIJKLMNOPQRSTUVWXYZabcdefghijklmnopqrstuv wxyz1234567890

Avenir Book

ABCDEFGHIJKLMNOPQRSTUVWXYZabcdefghijklmnopqrstuv wxyz1234567890

Avenir Medium

ABCDEFGHIJKLMNOPQRSTUVWXYZabcdefghijklmnopqrstuv wxyz1234567890

Avenir Medium Oblique

ABCDEFGHIJKLMNOPQRSTUVWXYZabcdefghijklmnopqrstuv wxyz1234567890

Avenir Black

ABCDEFGHIJKLMNOPQRSTUVWXYZabcdefghijklmnopqrst uvwxyz1234567890

Bauer Bodoni Roman

ABCDEFGHIJKLMNOPQRSTUVWXYZABCDEFGHIJKLMNOPQRSTUV WXYZ1234567890

Bauer Bodoni Italic

ABCDEFGHIJKLMNOPQRSTUVWXYZabcdefghijklmnopqrstuvwx yz1234567890

Bauer Bodoni Bold

ABCDEFGHIJKLMNOPQRSTUVWXYZabcdefghijklmnopqrs tuvwxyz1234567890

Bauer Bodoni Black

ABCDEFGHIJKLMNOPQRSTUVWXYZabcdefghijklmnopqr stuvwxyz1234567890

Bauer Bodoni Bold Condensed

ABCDEFGHIJKLMNOPQRSTUVWXYZabcedfghijklmnopqrstuvwxyz 1234567890

Bauer Bodoni Black Condensed

ABCDEFGHIJKLMNOPQRSTUVWXYZabcdefghijklmnopqrstuvwxyz 1234567890

Bembo Roman
ABCDEFGHIJKLMNOPQRSTUVWXYZabcdefghijklmnopqrstuvw
xyz1234567890

Bembo Italic
ABCDEFGHIJKLMNOPQRSTUVWXYZabcdefghijklmnopqrstuvwxyz
1234567890

Bembo Bold
ABCDEFGHIJKLMNOPQRSTUVWXYZabcdefghijklmnopqrs
tuvwxyz1234567890

Bembo Semibold
ABCDEFGHIJKLMNOPQRSTUVWXYZabcdefghijklmnopqrstu
vwxyz1234567890

Bembo Extra Bold
ABCDEFGHIJKLMNOPQRSTUVWXYZabcdefghijklmnop
qrstuvwxyz1234567890

ITC Benguiat Book
ABCDEFGHIJKLMNOPQRSTUVWXYZabcdefghijklmnopqrstu
vwxyz1234567890

ITC Benguiat Gothic Bold
ABCDEFGHIJKLMNOPQRSTUVWXYZabcdefghijklmnopqrs
tuvwxyz1234567890

ITC Berkeley Oldstyle Book
ABCDEFGHIJKLMNOPQRSTUVWXYZabcdefghijklmnopqrstuvwxyz
1234567890

ITC Berkeley Oldstyle Bold
ABCDEFGHIJKLMNOPQRSTUVWXYZabcdefghijklmnopqrstuvwxyz
1234567890

ITC Bodoni Book
ABCDEFGHIJKLMNOPQRSTUVWXYZabcdefghijklmnopqrstuvwxyz
1234567890

ITC Bodoni Book Italic
ABCDEFGHIJKLMNOPQRSTUVWXYZabcdefghijklmnopqrstuvwxyz
1234567890

ITC Bodoni Bold

ABCDEFGHIJKLMNOPQRSTUVWXYZabcdefghijklmnopqrstu vwxyz1234567890

ITC Bookman Roman

ABCDEFGHIJKLMNOPQRSTUVWXYZabcdefghijklmnopqr stuvwxyz1234567890

ITC Bookman Italic

ABCDEFGHIJKLMNOPQRSTUVWXYZabcdefghijklmnopqrst uvwxyz1234567890

ITC Bookman Bold

ABCDEFGHIJKLMNOPQRSTUVWXYZabcdefghijklmnopqr stuvwxyz1234567890

Century Old Style Roman

ABCDEFGHIJKLMNOPQRSTUVWXYZabcdefghijklmnopqrstuv wxyz1234567890

Century Old Style Italic

ABCDEFGHIJKLMNOPQRSTUVWXYZabcdefghijklmnopqrstuvwx yz1234567890

Century Old Style Bold

ABCDEFGHIJKLMNOPQRSTUVWXYZabcdefghijklmnopqr stuvwxyz1234567890

New Century Schoolbook Roman

ABCDEFGHIJKLMNOPQRSTUVWXYZabcdefghijklmnopqr stuvwxyz1234567890

New Century Schoolbook Italic

ABCDEFGHIJKLMNOPQRSTUVWXYZabcdefghijklmnopqr stuvwxyz1234567890

New Century Schoolbook Bold

ABCDEFGHIJKLMNOPQRSTUVWXYZabcdefghijklmn opqrstuvwxyz1234567890

Cheltenham Roman

ABCDEFGHIJKLMNOPQRSTUVWXYZabcdefghijklmnopqrstuv
wxyz1234567890

Cheltenham Italic

ABCDEFGHIJKLMNOPQRSTUVWXYZabcdefghijklmnopqrstuvwxyz
1234567890

Cheltenham Bold

ABCDEFGHIJKLMNOPQRSTUVWXYZabcdefghijklmnopqrst
uvwxyz1234567890

Clarendon Light

ABCDEFGHIJKLMNOPQRSTUVWXYZabcdefghijklmnopq
rstuvwxyz1234567890

Clarendon Roman

ABCDEFGHIJKLMNOPQRSTUVWXYZabcdefghijklmnopq
rstuvwxyz1234567890

Clarendon Bold

ABCDEFGHIJKLMNOPQRSTUVWXYZabcdefghijklmnop
qrstuvwxyz1234567890

Clearface Roman

ABCDEFGHIJKLMNOPQRSTUVWXYZabcdefghijklmnopqrstuvwxyz
1234567890

Clearface Italic

ABCDEFGHIJKLMNOPQRSTUVWXYZabcdefghijklmnopqrstuvwxyz
1234567890

Clearface Bold

ABCDEFGHIJKLMNOPQRSTUVWXYZabcdefghijklmnopqrstuvwxyz
1234567890

Clearface Heavy

ABCDEFGHIJKLMNOPQRSTUVWXYZabcdefghijklmnopqrstuvwxyz
1234567890

Clearface Black

ABCDEFGHIJKLMNOPQRSTUVWXYZabcdefghijklmnopqrstu
vwxyz1234567890

ITC Galliard Roman
ABCDEFGHIJKLMNOPQRSTUVWXYZabcdefghijklmnopqrstu
vwxyz1234567890

ITC Galliard Italic
ABCDEFGHIJKLMNOPQRSTUVWXYZabcdefghijklmnopqrstuv
wxyz1234567890

ITC Galliard Bold
ABCDEFGHIJKLMNOPQRSTUVWXYZabcdefghijklmnopq
rstuvwxyz1234567890

ITC Galliard Black
ABCDEFGHIJKLMNOPQRSTUVWXYZabcdefghijklmnop
qrstuvwxyz1234567890

ITC Galliard Ultra
ABCDEFGHIJKLMNOPQRSTUVWXYZabcdefghijklmno
pqrstuvwxyz1234567890

ITC Garamond Light
ABCDEFGHIJKLMNOPQRSTUVWXYZabcdefghijklmnopqrstuvwxyz
1234567890

ITC Garamond Light Italic
ABCDEFGHIJKLMNOPQRSTUVWXYZabcedfghijklmnopqrstuvwxyz
1234567890

ITC Garamond Book
ABCDEFGHIJKLMNOPQRSTUVWXYZabcdefghijklmnopqrstuvwxyz
1234567890

ITC Garamond Bold
ABCDEFGHIJKLMNOPQRSTUVWXYZabcdefghijklmnopqrstu
vwxyz1234567890

ITC Garamond Ultra
ABCDEFGHIJKLMNOPQRSTUVWXYZabcdefghijklmnopq
rstuvwxyz1234567890

ITC Garamond Light Condensed
ABCDEFGHIJKLMNOPQRSTUVWXYZabcdefghijklmnopqrstuvwxyz1234567890

ITC Garamond Book Condensed
ABCDEFGHIJKLMNOPQRSTUVWXYZabcdefghijklmnopqrstuvwxyz1234567890

ITC Garamond Bold Condensed
ABCDEFGHIJKLMNOPQRSTUVWXYZabcdefghijklmnopqrstuvwxyz
1234567890

ITC Garamond Ultra Condensed
ABCDEFGHIJKLMNOPQRSTUVWXYZabcdefghijklmnopqrstuvwxyz
1234567890

Glypha 35 Thin
ABCDEFGHIJKLMNOPQRSTUVWXYZabcdefghijklmnopqrstuvwxyz
1234567890

Glypha 45 Light
ABCDEFGHIJKLMNOPQRSTUVWXYZabcdefghijklmnopqrstuvwxyz
1234567890

Glypha 55 Regular
ABCDEFGHIJKLMNOPQRSTUVWXYZabcdefghijklmnopqrs
tuvwxyz1234567890

Glypha 55 Oblique
ABCDEFGHIJKLMNOPQRSTUVWXYZabcdefghijklmnopqrs
tuvwxyz1234567890

Glypha 65 Bold
ABCDEFGHIJKLMNOPQRSTUVWXYZabcdefghijklmnopqr
stuvwxyz1234567890

Glypha 75 Black
ABCDEFGHIJKLMNOPQRSTUVWXYZabcdefghijklmnopq
rstuvwxyz1234567890

Italia Book
ABCDEFGHIJKLMNOPQRSTUVWXYZabcdefghijklmnopqrstuvwxyz
1234567890

Italia Medium
ABCDEFGHIJKLMNOPQRSTUVWXYZabcdefghijklmnopqrstuvwx
yz1234567890

Italia Bold
ABCDEFGHIJKLMNOPQRSTUVWXYZabcdefghijklmnopqrstuvw
xyz1234567890

Janson Text Roman
ABCDEFGHIJKLMNOPQRSTUVWXYZabcdefghijklmnopqrst
uvwxyz1234567890

Janson Text Italic

ABCDEFGHIJKLMNOPQRSTUVWXYZabcdefghijklmnopqrstuvwxyz
1234567890

Janson Text Bold

ABCDEFGHIJKLMNOPQRSTUVWXYZabcdefghijklmnopq
rstuvwxyz1234567890

ITC Korinna Regular

ABCDEFGHIJKLMNOPQRSTUVWXYZabcdefghijklmnopqrstu
vwxyz1234567890

ITC Korinna Kursiv

ABCDEFGHIJKLMNOPQRSTUVWXYZabcdefghijklmnopqrstuv
wxyz1234567890

ITC Korinna Bold

ABCDEFGHIJKLMNOPQRSTUVWXYZabcdefghijklmnopqrst
uvwxyz1234567890

ITC Lubalin Graph Book

ABCDEFGHIJKLMNOPQRSTUVWXYZabcdefghijklmnopqrst
uvwxyz1234567890

ITC Lubalin Graph Demi

ABCDEFGHIJKLMNOPQRSTUVWXYZabcdefghijklmnopqrs
tuvwxyz1234567890

Melior Roman

ABCDEFGHIJKLMNOPQRSTUVWXYZabcdefghijklmnopqrstu
vwxyz1234567890

Melior Italic

ABCDEFGHIJKLMNOPQRSTUVWXYZabcdefghijklmnopqrstu
vwxyz1234567890

Melior Bold

ABCDEFGHIJKLMNOPQRSTUVWXYZabcdefghijklmnopqrst
uvwxyz1234567890

Memphis Light

ABCDEFGHIJKLMNOPQRSTUVWXYZabcdefghijklmnopqrstuv
wxyz1234567890

Memphis Medium
ABCDEFGHIJKLMNOPQRSTUVWXYZabcdefghijklmnopqrst
uvwxyz1234567890

Memphis Medium Italic
*ABCDEFGHIJKLMNOPQRSTUVWXYZabcdefghijklmnopqrstu
vwxyz1234567890*

Memphis Bold
**ABCDEFGHIJKLMNOPQRSTUVWXYZabcdefghijklmnopqrst
uvwxyz1234567890**

Memphis Extra Bold
**ABCDEFGHIJKLMNOPQRSTUVWXYZabcdefghijk
lmnopqrstuvwxyz1234567890**

Minion Roman
ABCDEFGHIJKLMNOPQRSTUVWXYZabcdefghijklmnopqrstuvwxyz
1234567890

Minion Italic
*ABCDEFGHIJKLMNOPQRSTUVWXYZabcdefghijklmnopqrstuvwxyz
1234567890*

Minion Semibold
**ABCDEFGHIJKLMNOPQRSTUVWXYZabcdefghijklmnopqrstuvwx
yz1234567890**

Minion Bold
**ABCDEFGHIJKLMNOPQRSTUVWXYZabcdefghijklmnopqrstuvwx
yz1234567890**

Minion Black
**ABCDEFGHIJKLMNOPQRSTUVWXYZabcdefghijklmnopqrstuvw
xyz1234567890**

ITC New Baskerville Roman
ABCDEFGHIJKLMNOPQRSTUVWXYZabcdefghijklmnopqrstuv
wxyz1234567890

ITC New Baskerville Italic
*ABCDEFGHIJKLMNOPQRSTUVWXYZabcdefghijklmnopqrstuvwxyz
1234567890*

ITC New Baskerville Bold
**ABCDEFGHIJKLMNOPQRSTUVWXYZabcdefghijklmnopqrstuv
wxyz1234567890**

Palatino Roman

ABCDEFGHIJKLMNOPQRSTUVWXYZabcdefghijklmnopqrstu
vwxyz1234567890

Palatino Italic

ABCDEFGHIJKLMNOPQRSTUVWXYZabcdefghijklmnopqrstuvw
xyz1234567890

Palatino Bold

ABCDEFGHIJKLMNOPQRSTUVWXYZabcdefghijklmnopqr
stuvwxyz1234567890

Plantin Light

ABCDEFGHIJKLMNOPQRSTUVWXYZabcdefghijklmnopqrs
tuvwxyz1234567890

Plantin Roman

ABCDEFGHIJKLMNOPQRSTUVWXYZabcdefghijklmnopqrs
tuvwxyz1234567890

Plantin Semibold

ABCDEFGHIJKLMNOPQRSTUVWXYZabcdefghijklmnop
qrstuvwxyz1234567890

Plantin Bold Condensed

ABCDEFGHIJKLMNOPQRSTUVWXYZabcdefghijklmnopqrstuvwxyz1234
567890

Poster Bodoni

ABCDEFGHIJKLMNOPQRSTUVWXYZabcdefghijkl
mnopqrstuvwxyz1234567890

Poster Bodoni Italic

ABCDEFGHIJKLMNOPQRSTUVWXYZabcdefghijkl
mnopqrstuvwxyz1234567890

Rockwell Light

ABCDEFGHIJKLMNOPQRSTUVWXYZabcdefghijklmnopqrstuvwxyz
1234567890

Rockwell Regular

ABCDEFGHIJKLMNOPQRSTUVWXYZabcdefghijklmnopqrstuv
wxyz1234567890

Rockwell Italic

ABCDEFGHIJKLMNOPQRSTUVWXYZabcdefghijklmnopqrstuvw xyz1234567890

Rockwell Bold

ABCDEFGHIJKLMNOPQRSTUVWXYZabcdefghijklmnopq rstuvwxyz1234567890

Rockwell Extra Bold

ABCDEFGHIJKLMNOPQRSTUVWXYZabcdefghijk lmnopqrstuvwxyz1234567890

Rockwell Condensed

ABCDEFGHIJKLMNOPQRSTUVWXYZabcdefghijklmnopqrstuvwxyz1234567890

Sabon Roman

ABCDEFGHIJKLMNOPQRSTUVWXYZabcdefghijklmnopqrstu vwxyz1234567890

Sabon Italic

ABCDEFGHIJKLMNOPQRSTUVWXYZabcdefghijklmnopqrst uvwxyz1234567890

Sabon Bold

ABCDEFGHIJKLMNOPQRSTUVWXYZabcdefghijklmnopqrst uvwxyz1234567890

Serifa Light

ABCDEFGHIJKLMNOPQRSTUVWXYZabcdefghijklmnopqrstuvwx yz1234567890

Serifa Roman

ABCDEFGHIJKLMNOPQRSTUVWXYZabcdefghijklmnopqrs tuvwxyz1234567890

Serifa Italic

ABCDEFGHIJKLMNOPQRSTUVWXYZabcdefghijklmnopqrst uvwxyz1234567890

Serifa Bold

ABCDEFGHIJKLMNOPQRSTUVWXYZabcdefghijklmnopq rstuvwxyz1234567890

Serifa Black

ABCDEFGHIJKLMNOPQRSTUVWXYZabcdefghijklmnop qrstuvwxyz1234567890

ITC Stone Serif Medium

ABCDEFGHIJKLMNOPQRSTUVWXYZabcdefghijklmnopqrstu
vwxyz1234567890

ITC Stone Serif Medium Italic

*ABCDEFGHIJKLMNOPQRSTUVWXYZabcdefghijklmnopqrstuvwx
yz1234567890*

ITC Stone Serif Semibold

**ABCDEFGHIJKLMNOPQRSTUVWXYZabcdefghijklmnopqrs
tuvwxyz1234567890**

ITC Stone Serif Bold

**ABCDEFGHIJKLMNOPQRSTUVWXYZabcdefghijklmn
opqrstuvwxyz1234567890**

Times Roman

ABCDEFGHIJKLMNOPQRSTUVWXYZabcdefghijklmnopqrstuvwxyz
1234567890

Times Italic

*ABCDEFGHIJKLMNOPQRSTUVWXYZabcdefghijklmnopqrstuvwxyz
1234567890*

Times Semibold

**ABCDEFGHIJKLMNOPQRSTUVWXYZabcdefghijklmnopqrstuv
wxyz1234567890**

Times Bold

**ABCDEFGHIJKLMNOPQRSTUVWXYZabcdefghijklmnopqrstuv
wxyz1234567890**

Times New Roman Regular

ABCDEFGHIJKLMNOPQRSTUVWXYZabcdefghijklmnopqrstuvwxyz
1234567890

Times New Roman Italic

*ABCDEFGHIJKLMNOPQRSTUVWXYZabcdefghijklmnopqrstuvwxyz
1234567890*

Times New Roman Bold

**ABCDEFGHIJKLMNOPQRSTUVWXYZabcdefghijklmnopqrstuv
wxyz1234567890**

ITC Weideman Book

ABCDEFGHIJKLMNOPQRSTUVWXYZabcdefghijklmnopqrstuvwxyz
1234567890

ITC Weideman Book Italic

ABCDEFGHIJKLMNOPQRSTUVWXYZabcdefghijklmnopqrstuvwxyz
1234567890

ITC Weideman Medium

ABCDEFGHIJKLMNOPQRSTUVWXYZabcdefghijklmnopqrstuvwxyz
1234567890

ITC Weideman Bold

ABCDEFGHIJKLMNOPQRSTUVWXYZabcdefghijklmnopqrstuvwx
yz1234567890

SANS SERIF

Akzidenz-Grotesque

ABCDEFGHIJKLMNOPQRSTUVWXYZabcdefghijklmnopqrstuvw
xyz1234567890

Akzidenz-Grotesque Light

ABCDEFGHIJKLMNOPQRSTUVWXYZabcdefghijklmnopqrstuvwxyz
1234567890

Akzidenz-Grotesque Bold

ABCDEFGHIJKLMNOPQRSTUVWXYZabcdefghijklmnopqrstuvw
xyz1234567890

Akzidenz-Grotesque Black

ABCDEFGHIJKLMNOPQRSTUVWXYZabcdefghijklmnopqr
stuvwxyz1234567890

Antique Olive Light

ABCDEFGHIJKLMNOPQRSTUVWXYZabcdefghijklmnopqrstuvwx
yz1234567890

Antique Olive Roman

ABCDEFGHIJKLMNOPQRSTUVWXYZabcdefghijklmnopqrst
uvwxyz1234567890

Antique Olive Bold

ABCDEFGHIJKLMNOPQRSTUVWXYZabcdefghijklmnopqrs
tuvwxyz1234567890

Arial Regular
ABCDEFGHIJKLMNOPQRSTUVWXYZabcdefghijklmnopqrstuvwxyz1234567890

Arial Light
ABCDEFGHIJKLMNOPQRSTUVWXYZabcdefghijklmnopqrstuvwxyz1234567890

Arial Medium
ABCDEFGHIJKLMNOPQRSTUVWXYZabcdefghijklmnopqrstuvwxyz1234567890

Arial Extra Bold
ABCDEFGHIJKLMNOPQRSTUVWXYZabcdefghijklmnopqrstuvwxyz1234567890

Arial Condensed
ABCDEFGHIJKLMNOPQRSTUVWXYZabcdefghijklmnopqrstuvwxyz1234567890

Arial Narrow Regular
ABCDEFGHIJKLMNOPQRSTUVWXYZabcdefghijklmnopqrstuvwxyz1234567890

Avant Garde
ABCDEFGHIJKLMNOPQRSTUVWXYZabcdefghijklmnopqrstuvwxyz1234567890

Avant Garde Extra Light
ABCDEFGHIJKLMNOPQRSTUVWXYZabcdefghijklmnopqrstuvwxyz1234567890

Avant Garde Book
ABCDEFGHIJKLMNOPQRSTUVWXYZabcdefghijklmnopqrstuvwxyz1234567890

Avant Garde Book Oblique
ABCDEFGHIJKLMNOPQRSTUVWXYZabcdefghijklmnopqrstuvwxyz1234567890

Avant Garde Medium
ABCDEFGHIJKLMNOPQRSTUVWXYZabcdefghijklmnopqrstuvwxyz1234567890

Avant Garde Demi
ABCDEFGHIJKLMNOPQRSTUVWXYZabcdefghijklmnopqrstuvwxyz1234567890

Avant Garde Bold

ABCDEFGHIJKLMNOPQRSTUVWXYZabcdefghijklmnopqr stuvwxyz1234567890

Avant Garde Condensed Book

ABCDEFGHIJKLMNOPQRSTUVWXYZabcdefghijklmnopqrstuvwxyz 1234567890

ITC Eras Light

ABCDEFGHIJKLMNOPQRSTUVWXYZabcdefghijklmnopqrstuvwxyz 1234567890

ITC Eras Book

ABCDEFGHIJKLMNOPQRSTUVWXYZabcdefghijklmnopqrstuvwxyz 1234567890

ITC Eras Medium

ABCDEFGHIJKLMNOPQRSTUVWXYZabcdefghijklmnopqrstuvwx yz1234567890

ITC Eras Demi

ABCDEFGHIJKLMNOPQRSTUVWXYZabcdefghijklmnopqrst uvwxyz1234567890

ITC Eras Bold

ABCDEFGHIJKLMNOPQRSTUVWXYZabcdefghijklmnopq rstuvwxyz1234567890

ITC Eras Ultra

ABCDEFGHIJKLMNOPQRSTUVWXYZabcdefghijklmn opqrstuvwxyz1234567890

Folio Light

ABCDEFGHIJKLMNOPQRSTUVWXYZabcdefghijklmnopqrstuvw xyz1234567890

Folio Medium

ABCDEFGHIJKLMNOPQRSTUVWXYZabcdefghijklmnopqrstuv wxyz1234567890

Folio Bold

ABCDEFGHIJKLMNOPQRSTUVWXYZabcdefghijklmn opqrstuvwxyz1234567890

Folio Extra Bold

ABCDEFGHIJKLMNOPQRSTUVWXYZabcdefghijklmno pqrstuvwxyz1234567890

Folio Bold Condensed
ABCDEFGHIJKLMNOPQRSTUVWXYZabcdefghijklmnopqrstuvwxyz1234567890

ITC Franklin Gothic Book
ABCDEFGHIJKLMNOPQRSTUVWXYZabcdefghijklmnopqrstuvwxyz
1234567890

ITC Franklin Gothic Book Italic
ABCDEFGHIJKLMNOPQRSTUVWXYZabcdefghijklmnopqrstuvwxyz
1234567890

ITC Franklin Gothic Demi
ABCDEFGHIJKLMNOPQRSTUVWXYZabcdefghijklmnopqrstuvwx
yz1234567890

ITC Franklin Gothic Heavy
ABCDEFGHIJKLMNOPQRSTUVWXYZabcdefghijklmnopqrstu
vwxyz1234567890

Friz Quadrata Regular
ABCDEFGHIJKLMNOPQRSTUVWXYZabcdefghijklmnopqrstuvwxyz
1234567890

Friz Quadrata Bold
ABCDEFGHIJKLMNOPQRSTUVWXYZabcdefghijklmnopqrstuvwxyz
1234567890

Frutiger Light
ABCDEFGHIJKLMNOPQRSTUVWXYZabcdefghijklmnopqrstuvwxyz
1234567890

Frutiger Regular
ABCDEFGHIJKLMNOPQRSTUVWXYZabcdefghijklmnopqrstuv
wxyz1234567890

Frutiger Regular Italic
ABCDEFGHIJKLMNOPQRSTUVWXYZabcdefghijklmnopqrstuv
wxyz1234567890

Frutiger Bold
ABCDEFGHIJKLMNOPQRSTUVWXYZabcdefghijklmnopqrstuv
wxyz1234567890

Frutiger Black
ABCDEFGHIJKLMNOPQRSTUVWXYZabcdefghijklmnopqr
stuvwxyz1234567890

Frutiger Ultra Black
**ABCDEFGHIJKLMNOPQRSTUVWXYZabcdefghijklm
nopqrstuvwxyz1234567890**

Futura Light
ABCDEFGHIJKLMNOPQRSTUVWXYZabcdefghijklmnopqrstuvwxyz
1234567890

Futura Book
ABCDEFGHIJKLMNOPQRSTUVWXYZabcdefghijklmnopqrstuvwxyz
1234567890

Futura Book Oblique
*ABCDEFGHIJKLMNOPQRSTUVWXYZabcdefghijklmnopqrstuv
wxyz1234567890*

Futura Bold
**ABCDEFGHIJKLMNOPQRSTUVWXYZabcdefghijklmnop
qrstuvwxyz1234567890**

Futura Heavy
**ABCDEFGHIJKLMNOPQRSTUVWXYZabcdefghijklmnopqrstuvwxyz
1234567890**

Futura Extra Bold
**ABCDEFGHIJKLMNOPQRSTUVWXYZabcdefghijklm
nopqrstuvwxyz1234567890**

Futura Condensed
ABCDEFGHIJKLMNOPQRSTUVWXYZabcdefghijklmnopqrstuvwxyz1234567890

Gil Sans Light
ABCDEFGHIJKLMNOPQRSTUVWXYZabcdefghijklmnopqrstuvwxyz
1234567890

Gil Sans Regular
ABCDEFGHIJKLMNOPQRSTUVWXYZabcdefghijklmnopqrstuvwxyz
1234567890

Gil Sans Italic
*ABCDEFGHIJKLMNOPQRSTUVWXYZabcdefghijklmnopqrstuvwxyz
1234567890*

Gil Sans Bold
**ABCDEFGHIJKLMNOPQRSTUVWXYZabcdefghijklmnopqr
stuvwxyz1234567890**

Gil Sans Extra Bold

ABCDEFGHIJKLMNOPQRSTUVWXYZabcdefghijklmn opqrstuvwxyz1234567890

Gil Sans Ultra Bold

ABCDEFGHIJKLMNOPQRSTUVWXYZabcdefghi jklmnopqrstuvwxyz1234567890

Helvetica Light

ABCDEFGHIJKLMNOPQRSTUVWXYZabcdefghijklmnopqrstuv wxyz1234567890

Helvetica Light Oblique

ABCDEFGHIJKLMNOPQRSTUVWXYZabcdefghijklmnopqrstuv wxyz1234567890

Helvetica Black

ABCDEFGHIJKLMNOPQRSTUVWXYZabcdefghijklm nopqrstuvwxyz1234567890

Helvetica Condensed

ABCDEFGHIJKLMNOPQRSTUVWXYZabcdefghijklmnopqrstuvwxyz 1234567890

Helvetica Compressed

ABCDEFGHIJKLMNOPQRSTUVWXYZabcdefghijklmnopqrstuvwxyz1234567890

Helvetica Rounded Bold

ABCDEFGHIJKLMNOPQRSTUVWXYZabcdefghijklmnopqr stuvwxyz1234567890

Helvetica Rounded Bold Oblique

ABCDEFGHIJKLMNOPQRSTUVWXYZabcdefghijklmnopqr stuvwxyz1234567890

Helvetica Rounded Black

ABCDEFGHIJKLMNOPQRSTUVWXYZabcdefghijklmn opqrstuvwxyz1234567890

Helvetica Rounded Bold Condensed

ABCDEFGHIJKLMNOPQRSTUVWXYZabcdefghijklmnopqrstuvwxyz 1234567890

Kabel Light

ABCDEFGHIJKLMNOPQRSTUVWXYZabcdefghijklmnopqrstuvwxyz 1234567890

Kabel Book
**ABCDEFGHIJKLMNOPQRSTUVWXYZabcdefghijklmnopqrstuvwxyz
1234567890**

Kabel Heavy
**ABCDEFGHIJKLMNOPQRSTUVWXYZabcdefghijklmnopqrstuvwx
yz1234567890**

Kabel Black
**ABCDEFGHIJKLMNOPQRSTUVWXYZabcdefghijklmnopqrstuvw
xyz1234567890**

Neue Helvetica Ultra Light
ABCDEFGHIJKLMNOPQRSTUVWXYZabcdefghijklmnopqrstuvwxyz
1234567890

Neue Helvetica Thin
ABCDEFGHIJKLMNOPQRSTUVWXYZabcdefghijklmnopqrstuvwxyz
1234567890

Neue Helvetica Light
ABCDEFGHIJKLMNOPQRSTUVWXYZabcdefghijklmnopqrstuvwx
yz1234567890

Neue Helvetica Medium
**ABCDEFGHIJKLMNOPQRSTUVWXYZabcdefghijklmnopqrstu
vwxyz1234567890**

Neue Helvetica Medium Italic
*ABCDEFGHIJKLMNOPQRSTUVWXYZabcdefghijklmnopqrstu
vwxyz1234567890*

Neue Helvetica Bold
**ABCDEFGHIJKLMNOPQRSTUVWXYZabcdefghijklmnopqrs
tuvwxyz1234567890**

Neue Helvetica Heavy
**ABCDEFGHIJKLMNOPQRSTUVWXYZabcdefghijklmnopqr
stuvwxyz1234567890**

Neue Helvetica Black
**ABCDEFGHIJKLMNOPQRSTUVWXYZabcdefghijklmnop
qrstuvwxyz1234567890**

Neue Helvetica Condensed
ABCDEFGHIJKLMNOPQRSTUVWXYZabcdefghijklmnopqrstuvwxyz1234567890

Neue Helvetica Extended
ABCDEFGHIJKLMNOPQRSTUVWXYZabcdefghijklmno
pqrstuvwxyz1234567890

News Gothic Regular
ABCDEFGHIJKLMNOPQRSTUVWXYZabcdefghijklmnopqrstuvwxyz
1234567890
News Gothic Italic
ABCDEFGHIJKLMNOPQRSTUVWXYZabcdefghijklmnopqrstuvwxyz
1234567890
News Gothic Bold
ABCDEFGHIJKLMNOPQRSTUVWXYZabcdefghijklmnopqrstuv
wxyz1234567890

Optima Regular
ABCDEFGHIJKLMNOPQRSTUVWXYZabcdefghijklmnopqrstuvw
xyz1234567890
Optima Oblique
ABCDEFGHIJKLMNOPQRSTUVWXYZabcdefghijklmnopqrstuvw
xyz1234567890
Optima Bold
ABCDEFGHIJKLMNOPQRSTUVWXYZabcdefghijklmnopqrstuvw
xyz1234567890

Agfa Rotis Sans Serif Light
ABCDEFGHIJKLMNOPQRSTUVWXYZabcdefghijklmnopqrstuvwxyz
1234567890
Agfa Rotis Sans Serif Regular
ABCDEFGHIJKLMNOPQRSTUVWXYZabcdefghijklmnopqrstuvwxyz
1234567890
Agfa Rotis Sans Serif Italic
ABCDEFGHIJKLMNOPQRSTUVWXYZabcdefghijklmnopqrstuvwxyz
1234567890
Agfa Rotis Sans Serif Bold
ABCDEFGHIJKLMNOPQRSTUVWXYZabcdefghijklmnopqrstuvwxyz
1234567890

Agfa Rotis Sans Serif Extra Bold
ABCDEFGHIJKLMNOPQRSTUVWXYZabcdefghijklmnopqrstuvwxyz
1234567890

Agfa Rotis Semisans Light
ABCDEFGHIJKLMNOPQRSTUVWXYZabcdefghijklmnopqrstuvwxyz
1234567890

Agfa Rotis Semisans Regular
ABCDEFGHIJKLMNOPQRSTUVWXYZabcdefghijklmnopqrstuvwxyz
1234567890

Agfa Rotis Semisans Italic
ABCDEFGHIJKLMNOPQRSTUVWXYZabcdefghijklmnopqrstuvwxyz
1234567890

Agfa Rotis Semisans Bold
ABCDEFGHIJKLMNOPQRSTUVWXYZabcdefghijklmnopqrstuvwxyz
1234567890

Agfa Rotis Semisans Extra Bold
ABCDEFGHIJKLMNOPQRSTUVWXYZabcdefghijklmnopqrstuvwxyz
1234567890

ITC Stone Sans Medium
ABCDEFGHIJKLMNOPQRSTUVWXYZabcdefghijklmnopqrstuvwx
yz1234567890

ITC Stone Sans Medium Italic
ABCDEFGHIJKLMNOPQRSTUVWXYZabcdefghijklmnopqrstuvwxyz
1234567890

ITC Stone Sans Semibold
ABCDEFGHIJKLMNOPQRSTUVWXYZabcdefghijklmnopqrstu
vwxyz1234567890

ITC Stone Sans Bold
ABCDEFGHIJKLMNOPQRSTUVWXYZabcdefghijklmnopqr
stuvwxyz1234567890

ITC Symbol Book
ABCDEFGHIJKLMNOPQRSTUVWXYZabcdefghijklmnopqrstuvw
xyz1234567890

ITC Symbol Book Italic
ABCDEFGHIJKLMNOPQRSTUVWXYZabcdefghijklmnopqrstuvwxyz
1234567890

ITC Symbol Medium
ABCDEFGHIJKLMNOPQRSTUVWXYZabcdefghijklmnopqrstu
vwxyz1234567890

ITC Symbol Bold
ABCDEFGHIJKLMNOPQRSTUVWXYZabcdefghijklmnopqrs
tuvwxyz1234567890

ITC Symbol Black
ABCDEFGHIJKLMNOPQRSTUVWXYZabcdefghijklmno
pqrstuvwxyz1234567890

Trade Gothic Light
ABCDEFGHIJKLMNOPQRSTUVWXYZabcdefghijklmnopqrstuvwxyz
1234567890

Trade Gothic Regular
ABCDEFGHIJKLMNOPQRSTUVWXYZabcdefghijklmnopqrstuvwxyz
1234567890

Trade Gothic Oblique
ABCDEFGHIJKLMNOPQRSTUVWXYZabcdefghijklmnopqrstuvwxyz
1234567890

Trade Gothic Bold
ABCDEFGHIJKLMNOPQRSTUVWXYZabcdefghijklmnopqrstuvwxyz1234
567890

Trade Gothic Bold No. 2
ABCDEFGHIJKLMNOPQRSTUVWXYZabcdefghijklmnopqrstuvwxyz
1234567890

Trade Gothic Condensed
ABCDEFGHIJKLMNOPQRSTUVWXYZabcdefghijklmnopqrstuvwxyz1234567890

Univers 45 Light
ABCDEFGHIJKLMNOPQRSTUVWXYZabcdefghijklmnopqrstuv
wxyz1234567890

Univers 55

ABCDEFGHIJKLMNOPQRSTUVWXYZabcdefghijklmnopqrst
uvwxyz1234567890

Univers 55 Oblique

*ABCDEFGHIJKLMNOPQRSTUVWXYZabcdefghijklmnopqrst
uvwxyz1234567890*

Univers 65 Bold

**ABCDEFGHIJKLMNOPQRSTUVWXYZabcdefghijklmnopqrst
uvwxyz1234567890**

Univers 75 Black

**ABCDEFGHIJKLMNOPQRSTUVWXYZabcdefghijklmn
opqrstuvwxyz1234567890**

Univers 57 Condensed

ABCDEFGHIJKLMNOPQRSTUVWXYZabcdefghijklmnopqrstuvwxyz
1234567890

Univers 53 Extended

ABCDEFGHIJKLMNOPQRSTUVWXYZabcdefghij
klmnopqrstuvwxyz1234567890

○ Chapter 6: Grid Design Basics

Grids use vertical and horizontal thresholds to indicate divisions of space and to provide a way for designers to determine how the interior proportions of a page should be used. They provide a structure within which to organize both text and image and allow diverse compositional elements to exist in a layout with a degree of order and visual harmony.

TYPES OF GRIDS

Grids come in many different forms. When creating a grid system, designers may use their intuition, or they may base the grid on established rules of space or commonly used sizing systems such as square or double square, and the European proportion of A paper sizes. Grids can be created with specific content in mind or as part of a system that is designed to give unity to diverse content. They are expandable and can be made up of equal unit sections, or can be composed from a combination of units of varying proportion. In some cases, two or more grid systems can be used together for one document or several rela-ted grids may be used for deliverables that are part of a series.

Defining Variables

Grids systems can be used to define the following variables: margin width, proportion of areas on a page, number and size of columns, position of images, headings, body text, and the placement of folios and footnotes.

Uses for Grids

Books, magazines, Web pages, annual reports, brochures, timetables, posters, catalogs, advertising campaigns, and signage systems all benefit from the use of a grid system.

Why use a Grid?

One benefit of using grids is that they can create a sense of continuity across a sequence of pages or a range of deliverables in the same campaign or series. Another is speed; grids are a powerful tool for organizing information and laying out pages quickly. Finally, in the case of single-page compositions, they can help a designer create visual harmony and aesthetically connect diverse compositional elements.

Grids are not only a valuable tool for designers, they are also useful to readers/viewers. In sequential documents, the use of an organizational system allows viewers to move through content easily. This is especially true of layouts that contain a combination of complex visual elements.

ANATOMY OF A GRID

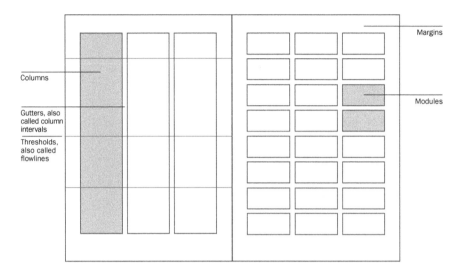

Margins

Columns

Gutters, also
called column
intervals

Thresholds,
also called
flowlines

Modules

WORKING WITH GRIDS

One of the most common misconceptions about grids is that they produce highly structured layouts and stifle intuition and originality. By working with grids, it is possible for designers to create aesthetically pleasing and visually arresting work. Grids can be as flexible as you want them to be. If the project demands it, they can help a designer produce an ordered conservative layout, but they also can provide a starting point to create exciting and experimental design work. To avoid feeling stifled by a grid, it is important to remember that a designer may re-create, alter, and at times even break the rules of the grid that he or she has designed.

Symmetry Versus Asymmetry

One of the first questions to ask when developing a grid system is whether a symmetrical or asymmetrical grid is more appropriate. There are advantages to both, and the determination should be made based on the content and visual tone required for a particular project.

A symmetrical grid is most often used for text-heavy books or publications. It is an ideal format to choose when one wants the most uniformity in a page layout.

An example of a symmetrical spread with margins set.

Asymmetrical grids are most useful when one wants layouts to vary across pages and when there is a range of elements (images, footnotes, sidebar text, etc) that must be included in a layout.

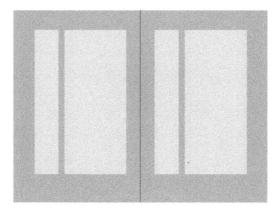

An example of an asymmetrical page layout with margins set.

Margins and Grids

The size and placement of margins is one of the first variables that affect the way viewers experience content. Generous margins give pages an open feel and accommodate a large amount of white space. Tighter margins allow for inclusion of more content but can lead to pages that appear to be packed with text and imagery. For novels and text-heavy books, smaller margins are often appropriate. Annual reports, photography books, and brochures are usually better served by wider margins.

In either case, it is important to give sufficient space both for the outside margins (so that a reader's thumbs don't cover content as they hold a book or brochure) and for the gutter and spine.

This is an example of a page layout with tighter margins. In such a system, a large amount of content can be placed on pages and effective use of white space will be determined by the designer's placement of elements within the composition.

Here is an example of a spread with larger margins. This layout system will accommodate less content but is likely to result in a visually open design.

Things to Consider Before Constructing a Grid

Does the grid need to accommodate headers or footers?

Will sidebars be needed?

How many columns will be appropriate?

Would content be best served by a more rigid or a looser grid system?

Does it make sense to base the grid on the content or some element of the content?

Are you most comfortable working with a mathematically or intuitively constructed grid?

Creating a Grid Using Graphic Software

Grids are most easily created in page layout programs (such as Adobe InDesign and QuarkXPress) by dragging guides to appropriate positions in the Master Page layout view. Page margins, the number of columns, and gutter width should be determined in the Document Setup window. In other graphics programs, such as Adobe Photoshop and Illustrator, one may want to create the grid on a new layer so that it can be edited separately from the content. Some designers find that using guides for proportions of the grid is sufficient; others like to actually draw out lines on a different layer or on the master page.

Steps to Making a Grid

1. Identify the type of grid that will be most appropriate for the content
   a. Symmetrical or Asymmetrical
   b. Constructional, Typographic, Hierarchical, or Modular

2. Choose type size, leading, font etc, so that the grid does not conflict with the other design decisions that you make.

3. Determine page size based on the content or the client brief (create new page in Document Setup).

4. Decide how many columns or units should be included in the grid and the size of the gutter between columns.

5. Define the margins of the page and the proportion of columns on the page (in Document Setup).

6. Position primary alignment points (using guides).

7. Add and position additional thresholds (using guides).

8. Test grid by laying out several pages with sample of content.

9. Make necessary revisions based on how grids work with given content.

Constructional Grids

A constructional grid refers to a loose structural system that is based on placement of compositional elements and their relation to each other. Unlike other types of grids, constructional grids are not created before one begins to layout content. Instead, the designer starts by positioning elements on a page in order of importance. Thresholds and alignment points are created as each item is placed and repositioned on the page. It may be possible for a viewer to recognize that common thresholds have been used in a layout that was made with a constructional grid, however sometimes only the designer will be able to identify how relational placement helped to create the resulting composition.

Since this system is so loose, some designers may not recognize constructional grids as grids at all. They may prefer to see their decisions as derived from intuition rather than structure. Whether one uses the term constructional grid or not is largely irrelevant, however understanding that this technique is a way to organize content can be helpful when one starts working with complex combinations of type and image.

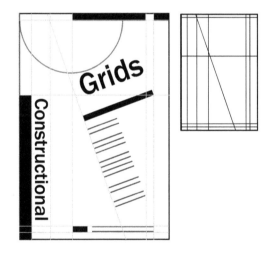

Constructional grids are a good option for designers who feel constrained or uncomfortable using a static grid system as well as for compositions that are not part of a sequential document. They allow for variety across pages or within a single composition and almost always result in an asymmetrical layout.

TYPOGRAPHIC UNIT GRIDS

These grids are based on the unit of text type and space between lines (also called linespacing or leading). Units are made functional by placing elements in the framework that has been created using typographic proportions.

Before constructing a typographic unit grid, the designer should choose page size, margin widths, typeface, point size, linespacing, and line length.

Typographic unit grids are most useful when working on documents that need to include a large amount of text. They allow the designer to use baselines to easily align body text with sidebars or caption text.

One problem with typographic unit grids is that the individual modules are so small that often they give very little indication as to where to place larger or repeating elements. They are often more effective when combined with a composite grid (see facing page).

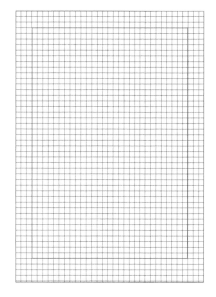

This typographic unit grid was made using the linespacing created by 10 point Helvetica with 2 points of leading. To make a typographic unit grid in a page layout program like QuarkXPress or Adobe InDesign, one should turn on the baseline grid and make sure that the page margins will correctly accommodate the linespacing that has been chosen. Then guides can be placed vertically at the same intervals as the space between baselines.

COMPOSITE GRIDS

Composite grids primarily define structural thresholds and alignment points and can be applied to an existing typographic unit grid to give a designer additional indication of where to place content within a sequential document. A composite grid may indicate the placement of columns, page headers, folios, notes etc.

The benefit of adding a composite grid to the typographic unit grid is that it includes primary flow lines and can make laying out pages easier. The combination of a composite grid with a typographic unit grid easily accommodates both text and other visual elements.

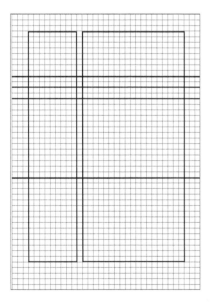

This example shows what the typographic unit grid on the opposite page would look like with flow lines (or thresholds) added.

4

Constraints

Constraints – grids can be seen as limiting, however designers work with constraints all the time. Whether deadlines, budget, color or type choices; designers excel in when given structure. Grids are simply self-imposed parameters that can help a designer create layouts with consistency and flow with in a particular framework. There are as many opportunities as there are constraints that created by working with a grid.

Grids Can Be Used For:	Arbitrary Decisions: Whether one creates a grid based on intuition or uses pre-existing unit structures or sizes, a grid can help a designer make decisions that follow a form and feel less arbitrary. This can be helpful both in the creative process and when explaining design decisions to clients.
Books	
magazines	
web-pages	
annual reports	
brochures	
timetables	Grids can be seen as limiting, however designers work with constraints all the time. Whether deadlines, budget, color or type choices; designers excel in when given structure.
posters	
catalogues	
advertising campaigns	
Types of Grids:	Grids can allow a designer to create a multitude of layouts that use a range of different visual elements from a single framework
Constructional	
Compositional	
Modular	When creating a grid system a designer may use his/her intuition or s/he may base the grid on established rules of space or commonly used system such as: square and double square, A paper size.
Equal Unit	
Hierarchical	

24

In these examples, it is possible to see what the combined typographic unit and composite grid would look like with content added.

MODULAR GRIDS

Originally developed in the 1950s and 1960s by Swiss designers Karl Gerstner, Emil Ruder, and Josef Müller-Brockmann, modular grids are still used by contemporary designers who are looking for flexible systems in which to order content.

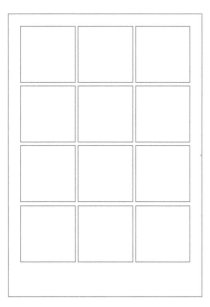

Modular grids are made of units of equal size with the proportions decided on by the designer. Units can be squares or rectangles.

Modular grids divide a page into equally proportioned horizontal and vertical units. These modules help indicate where text and images should be placed on a page. Room is left between modules so that there is space for gutters if several units are combined into a single column. Working with a modular grid gives a designer added flexibility because there are numerous flow lines on which visual elements can be aligned. Modular grids are well suited for multipage documents such as magazines, books, catalogs, and annual reports.

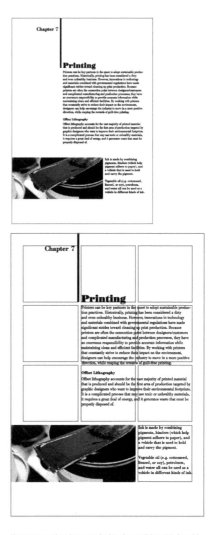

Here, content has been applied to the modular grid. An odd number of horizontal units makes it easier to accommodate body text with captions and images in a composition.

HIERARCHICAL GRIDS

Hierarchical grids are used when a specific division of space is needed across multiple pages. Hierarchical grids are ideal for use on websites and may replace or be used in addition to wireframes (see page 195) for some jobs.

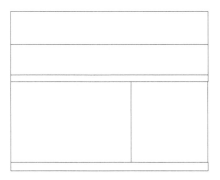

Hierarchical grid showing the division of space on a proposed webpage

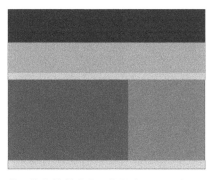

Hierarchical grid with shading added to denote areas of importance on the page. Shading is most helpful to the designer or design team. It is unlikely that this type of grid will be shown to clients.

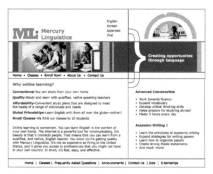

This image shows what a hierarchical grid would look like with content added.

Hierarchical grids can be made by dividing a page into fields or content areas (usually shown as rectangles) based on the relative importance of content. It is often helpful to use several shades of color or gray to visually denote the importance of content fields. Hierarchical grids can be made in any graphics program by positioning rectangles of color over the proportions of an intended page. Hierarchical grids are most useful when a high degree of consistency is required across a sequence of pages. This includes navigation and header areas that usually appear in the same place on each page on a website. When constructing a hierarchical grid, shading and tone may be used to indicate areas where content varies from page to page.

○ Chapter 7: Paper

NORTH AMERICAN SHEET SIZES

Most paper manufactured and sold in North America is measured in inches. Sheet sizes are based on trimming a quantity of 8½" × 11" (216 × 279 mm) items or pages from a single sheet with a minimum of waste. Some sheet sizes, such as 11" × 17" (279 × 432 mm), are exact multiples of the 8½" × 11" (216 × 279 mm) inch standard. Other sheet sizes are also based on multiples of 8½" × 11" (216 × 279 mm), but are slightly oversized to accommodate on-press requirements. For instance, a 23" × 35" (584 × 889 mm) inch sheet would yield sixteen trimmed 8½" × 11" (216 × 279 mm) flyers or a sixteen-page signature while allowing a narrow margin for bleeds, grippers, and color bars.

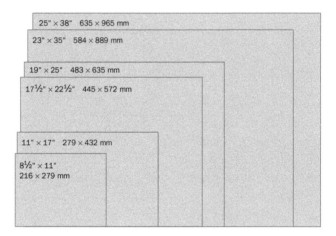

Printers in North America use sheets measured in inches with sizes based on multiples of 8½" × 11" (216 × 279 mm) inches.

NORTH AMERICAN SHEET SIZES AND METRIC EQUIVALENTS

Size (inches)	Size (millimeters)
8½ × 11	216 × 279
11 × 17	279 × 432
17½ × 22½	445 × 572
19 × 25	483 × 635
23 × 35	584 × 889
25 × 38	635 × 965

INTERNATIONAL, OR ISO, SHEET SIZES

Papers manufactured and sold outside of North America are based on 1 square meter. The International Standards Organization (ISO) system of paper sizes applies to all grades of paper and paper board and consists of five series of sizes: A, RA, SR, B, and C. Within each series, each sheet is twice the size of the next smaller sheet and half the size of the next larger sheet.

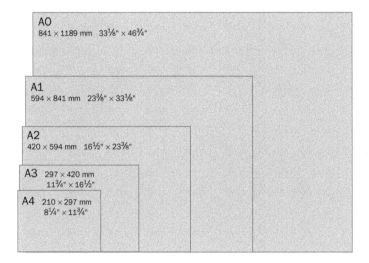

The starting point for ISO sizes is the A0 sheet, which measures 841 × 1189 mm (33 1/8" × 46 3/4") and has an area of 1 square meter. Each smaller size is a fraction of the A0 size. For instance, the A1 size (594 × 841 mm) is half of A0, and the A2 (420 × 594 mm) is one quarter of A0. Sizes larger than A0 retain the same proportions and a numeral prefix is added to the letter. For example, a 2A0 sheet is twice the size (1189 × 1682 mm) of an A0 sheet. The A series is used for general printed matter, including letterhead and publications.

ISO A SHEET SIZES AND INCH EQUIVALENTS

ISO Size	Size (millimeters)	Size (inches) approx.
4A0	1682 × 2378	66¼ × 93⅜
2A0	1189 × 1682	25½ × 36⅛
A0	841 × 1189	33⅛ × 46¾
A1	594 × 841	23⅜ × 33⅛
A2	420 × 594	16½ × 23⅜
A3	297 × 420	11¾ × 16½
A4	210 × 297	8¼ × 11¼
A5	148 × 210	5⅞ × 8¼
A6	105 × 148	4⅛ × 5⅞
A7	74 × 105	2⅞ × 4⅛
A8	52 × 74	2 × 2⅞

In addition to the preceding A sizes, there are two series from which A sizes can be cut. The series prefixed R and SR are designated as parent sheets for A sizes with tolerances for accommodating bleeds and extra trims.

ISO R and SR Sheet Sizes and Inch Equivalents

ISO Size	Size (millimeters)	Size (inches) approx.
RA0	860 × 1220	33⅞ × 48⅛
RA1	610 × 860	24⅛ × 33⅞
RA2	430 × 610	17 × 24
SRA0	900 × 128	35½ × 50⅜
SRA1	640 × 900	25¼ × 35½
SRA2	450 × 640	17⅞ × 25¼

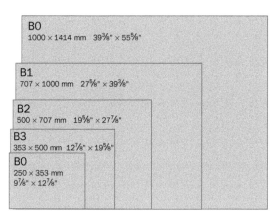

The B series is about half way between two A sizes and is intended as an alternative to the A sheets. ISO B series sheets are narrower than the A series and are usually used for posters and wall charts. The B series is based on a B0 size of 1000 × 1414 mm.

ISO B Sheet Sizes and Inch Equivalents

ISO Size	Size (millimeters)	Size (inches) approx.
B0	1000 × 1414	39⅜ × 55⅝
B1	707 × 1000	27⅞ × 39⅜
B2	500 × 707	19⅝ × 27⅞
B3	353 × 500	12⅞ × 19⅝
B4	250 × 353	9⅞ × 12⅞
B5	176 × 250	7 × 9⅞
B6	125 × 176	5 × 7
B7	88 × 125	3½ × 5
B8	62 × 88	2½ × 3½

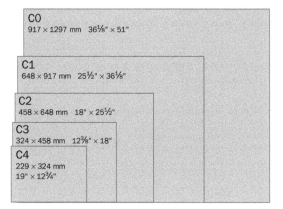

C0
917 × 1297 mm   36⅛" × 51"

C1
648 × 917 mm   25½" × 36⅛"

C2
458 × 648 mm   18" × 25½"

C3
324 × 458 mm   12⅜" × 18"

C4
229 × 324 mm
19" × 12¾"

The C series is used for folders, postcards, and envelopes suitable for stationery in the A sizes. (For more information on the C series as it pertains to envelopes, see Chapter 8, Envelopes and Folders.)

ISO C Sheet Sizes and Inch Equivalents

ISO Size	Size (millimeters)	Size (inches) approx.
C0	917 × 1297	36⅛ × 51
C1	648 × 917	25½ × 36⅛
C2	458 × 648	18 × 25
C3	324 × 458	12¾ × 18
C4	229 × 324	9 × 12½
C5	162 × 229	6⅜ × 9
C6	114 × 162	4½ × 6⅜
C7	81 × 114	3¼ × 4½
C8	57 × 81	2¼ × 3¼

BASIS WEIGHT EQUIVALENTS

In North America, the term *basis weight* or *ream weight* is used to define the weight in pounds of a ream of paper cut to a given size. (A ream is defined a 500 sheets of the basic size of a paper.) Basis weight is stated in pounds as represented by the # symbol.

The basic size of a sheet varies according to its grade. (Note that the basic size is only one of many standard sizes for each grade and is only used as a means of determining basis weight.) Basic sizes used to determine basis weight of some common papers are listed below:

Paper type	Sheet size (inches)	Sheet size (millimeters)
Bond, ledger, and writing	17 × 22	432 × 559
Uncoated book and text	25 × 38	635 × 965
Coated book	25 × 38	635 × 965
Cover	20 × 26	508 × 660
Bristol	22½ × 28½	572 × 724
Kraft, tag, and newsprint	24 × 36	610 × 914

Because of the size variations, paper grades that share the same basis weight may not look and feel as though they share the same basis weight. For instance, when comparing a sheet of 65# text and 65# cover stock, the cover stock will look and feel much heavier.

The following list of equivalents should help to define the basis weight differences between various grades.

Paper grade	Equivalent to
16# bond	40# text
20# bond	50# text
24# bond	60# text
28# bond	70# text
90# text	50# cover
100# text	55# cover
110# text	60# cover
120# text	65# cover

GRAMMAGE

Outside of North America, the weight of paper is measured in grams per square meter (gsm). The grammage system measures the weights of all papers without taking into consideration their size or grade. This system standardizes a ream at 500 sheets and defines a sheet as 1 square meter (A size). The term grammage is used to define the basis weight of all grades of paper measured in grams per square meter.

The following list gives some basis weight and grammage equivalents. Because North American basis weights are based on different basic sizes, the progression of weight conversion may not seem to be as logical as the basis weight comparisons on the opposite page.

Paper grade	Equivalent to	Paper grade	Equivalent to
16# bond	59 gsm	60# cover	162 gsm
24# bond	89 gsm	65# cover	176 gsm
		80# cover	216 gsm
67# bristol	148 gsm	100# cover	270 gsm
80# bristol	178 gsm	120# cover	325 gsm
100# bristol	219 gsm		
120# bristol	263 gsm	90# index	163 gsm
140# bristol	307 gsm	110# index	199 gsm
		140# index	253 gsm
30# text	44 gsm	170# index	308 gsm
40# text	59 gsm		
45# text	67 gsm		
60# text	89 gsm		
70# text	104 gsm		
80# text	118 gsm		
100# text	148 gsm		

Converting Basis Weight to Grammage

To convert the basis weight of a paper to its grammage, look up the sheet size in the left-hand column of the chart below. "lb." means pounds (basis weight).

Size	Basis weight to grammage	Grammage to basis weight
17" × 22" (432 × 559 mm)	3.760 × lb. = gsm	0.266 × gsm = lb.
20" × 26" (508 × 660 mm)	2.704 × lb. = gsm	0.370 × gsm = lb.
22" × 28" (559 × 711 mm)	2.282 × lb. = gsm	0.438 × gsm = lb.
22½" × 28½" (572 × 724 mm)	2.195 × lb. = gsm	0.456 × gsm = lb.
24" × 36" (610 × 914 mm)	1.627 × lb. = gsm	0.614 × gsm = lb.
25" × 38" (635 × 965 mm)	1.48 × lb. = gsm	0.675 × gsm = lb.

CALIPER, BULK, AND PPI

Paper thickness is defined as caliper. Caliper is measured in thousandths of an inch and expressed as point size. One point equals 0.001 inch. Stock that is 0.007 inch thick is described as 7 point or 7 pt. Points are most often used when referring to cover stock. It is also used by the U.S. Postal Service, which states its thickness requirements in calipers.

The term *bulk* is used to refer to the thickness of paper relative to its paper weight. A paper's finish will have an impact on its bulk. For instance, coated papers tend to be thinner than uncoated papers and have less bulk for their basis weight.

Publishers often state bulk as pages per inch, or ppi. Below is a comparison chart that compares caliper size with pages per inch.

Caliper	Pages per inch (ppi)
0.0020	1000
0.0024	842
0.0028	726
0.0034	592
0.0038	532
0.0042	470
0.0046	432
0.0050	400
0.0054	372
0.0060	332

BASIS WEIGHT/CALIPER EQUIVALENTS

The following chart gives an approximate caliper thickness for the different basis weights of some common papers. Because a paper's finish also affects its thickness or bulk, calipers are also given for common finishes.

Basis Weight	Coated	Smooth	Vellum	Textured
Bond/Writing				
13#		0.0021	0.0025	0.0027
16#		0.0026	0.0031	0.0033
20#		0.0032	0.0039	0.0042
24#		0.0038	0.0047	0.0050
Index				
90#		0.0080	0.0084	
110#		0.0096	0.0104	
140#		0.0132	0.0140	
170#		0.0144	0.0160	
Book/Text				
40#		0.0025	0.0031	0.0034
50#	0.0023	0.0031	0.0038	0.0041
60#	0.0028	0.0038	0.0046	0.0050
70#	0.0034	0.0044	0.0054	0.0058
80#	0.0040	0.0050	0.0059	0.0065
90#	0.0046	0.0057	0.0065	0.0074
100#	0.0052	0.0063	0.0071	0.0082
120#	0.0060	0.0076	0.0082	0.0100
Cover				
50#		0.0058	0.0070	0.0075
80#	0.0072	0.0093	0.0113	0.0120
100#	0.0092	0.0116	0.0140	0.0150

PPI FORMULA

Determining pages per inch can be important for determining the thickness of a finished publication. To calculate the number of pages per inch, calculate the caliper (points) of eight pages (four sheets) then divide the number of points into eight. In the following example, four sheets of a hypothetical paper measures 0.016 inch in thickness.

Example: 8.000 ÷ 0.016 = 500 ppi

FINISHES

In addition to considering basis weight or grammage, caliper, and sheet size, paper comes in finishes that range from smooth to textured. Uncoated papers also come in an assortment of finishes that are embossed into the paper as it is dried. These include linen, laid, and cockle textures.

Coated papers are available in uncalendered (an unpolished coated surface), machine calendered (a smoother finish), and supercalendared (highly polished) finishes—processes that affect the smoothness or glossiness of the surface. These can range from a matte or dull-coat finish to the high-gloss sheen of a cast-coated stock.

GRAIN

Grain refers to the alignment of the fibers on a given sheet of paper. The grain direction of a paper can affect folding accuracy and degree of stiffness. Paper tears and folds more easily when it is torn or folded with the direction of the grain. Folding paper against the grain can result in a rough or uneven fold. Business cards cut so that the length of the card runs in the direction of the grain tend to feel flimsier than cards cut with their length against the grain. It's best to check with your printer to determine the best way to set up your document for optimum grain direction.

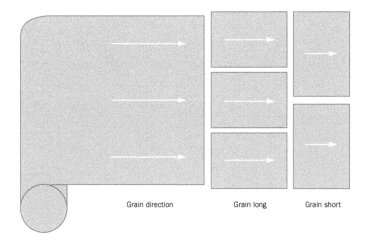

Grain direction   Grain long   Grain short

Paper is manufactured on rolls with the fibers aligned parallel to the edge of the roll. Sheets are cut from these rolls. When fibers are parallel to the length of the sheet, the stock is described as grain long. When fibers run parallel to the width of a sheet, the stock is grain short. Grain direction can affect printing stability, and long-grain sheets are generally preferred for multicolored jobs. Printing press sizes can sometimes necessitate the use of short-grained paper, so it's best to check with your printer before preparing your files.

Getting the Most from a Sheet

Minimizing wasted trim involves understanding how many trimmed pages will fit on a standard paper size. Use the following chart to determine how many pages will fit on North American standard paper sizes. (Note: Trim size does not include bleed allowances.)

Trimmed Page Size of Finished Piece (inches and millimeters)	Number of Pages in Finished Piece	Number of Finished Pieces from Each Sheet	Paper Size (inches and millimeters)
9 × 12	16	2	38 × 50 (965 × 1269 mm)
(228.6 × 304.8 mm)	8	2	25 × 38 (635 × 965 mm)
	4	4	25 × 38 (635 × 965 mm)
8½ × 11	16	2	35 × 45 (888 × 1142 mm)
(215.9 × 279.4 mm)	8	2	23 × 35 (584 × 888 mm)
	4	4	23 × 35 (584 × 888 mm)
8 × 10	4	8	35 × 45 (888 × 1142 mm)
(203.2 × 254 mm)	8	4	35 × 45 (888 × 1142 mm)
	16	2	35 × 45 (888 × 1142 mm)
6 × 9	32	2	38 × 50 (965 × 1269 mm)
(152.4 × 228.6 mm)	16	2	25 × 38 (635 × 965 mm)
	8	4	25 × 38 (635 × 965 mm)
	4	8	25 × 38 (635 × 965 mm)
6 × 4½	32	2	25 × 38 (635 × 965 mm)
(152.4 × 114.3 mm)	16	4	25 × 38 (635 × 965 mm)
	8	8	25 × 38 (635 × 965 mm)
	4	16	25 × 38 (635 × 965 mm)
5 × 8	4	16	35 × 45 (888 × 1142 mm)
(127 × 203.2 mm)	8	8	35 × 45 (888 × 1142 mm)
	32	2	35 × 45 (888 × 1142 mm)
4¼ × 5⅜	32	4	35 × 45 (888 × 1142 mm)
(107.95 × 136.53 mm)	16	8	35 × 45 (888 × 1142 mm)
	8	16	35 × 45 (888 × 1142 mm)
	4	32	35 × 45 (888 × 1142 mm)
4 × 9	24	2	25 × 38 (635 × 965 mm)
(101.6 × 228.6 mm)	16	6	38 × 50 (965 × 1269 mm)
	12	4	25 × 38 (635 × 965 mm)
	8	12	38 × 50 (965 × 1269 mm)
	4	12	25 × 38 (635 × 965 mm)

PAPER ESTIMATOR

Consult the chart for determining how many pieces can be cut from a single sheet of paper (see page 67), then refer to this chart for estimating the amount of paper needed for a given quantity. To determine how many sheets of paper will be needed for a job, check the number that will fit on a single sheet in the left-hand column. Then find the corresponding quantity by reading across on the top column (Example: If 16 pieces will fit on a single sheet, printing a quantity of 3,000 would require 188 sheets of paper.) Note that quantities given do not account for spoilage. Spoilage percentages are usually determined by individual printers, depending on the length and complexity of the press run and the complexity of the binding process.

Number Out of Sheet	Press Run 500	1M	1.5M	2M	2.5M	3M	3.5M	4M	4.5M	5M
2	250	500	750	1000	1250	1500	1750	2000	2250	2500
3	167	334	500	667	834	1000	1167	1334	1500	1667
4	125	250	375	500	625	750	875	1000	1125	1250
5	100	200	300	400	500	600	700	800	900	1000
6	84	167	250	334	417	599	584	667	750	834
7	72	143	215	286	358	429	500	572	643	715
8	63	125	188	250	313	375	438	500	563	625
9	56	112	167	223	278	334	389	445	500	556
10	50	100	150	200	250	300	350	400	450	500
11	46	91	137	182	228	273	319	364	410	455
12	42	84	126	168	209	250	292	334	375	417
13	39	77	116	154	193	231	270	308	347	385
14	36	72	108	144	179	215	250	286	322	358
15	34	67	100	134	167	200	234	267	300	334
16	32	63	94	125	157	188	219	250	282	313
17	30	59	89	118	148	177	206	236	265	295
18	28	56	84	112	139	167	195	223	250	279
19	27	53	79	106	132	156	185	211	237	264
20	25	50	75	100	125	150	175	200	225	250
21	24	48	72	96	120	143	167	191	216	239
22	23	46	69	91	114	137	160	182	205	228
23	22	44	66	87	109	131	153	174	196	218
24	21	42	63	84	105	126	146	167	186	209
25	20	40	60	80	100	120	140	160	180	200
26	20	39	58	77	97	116	135	154	174	193
27	19	38	56	75	93	112	130	149	167	186
28	18	36	54	72	90	108	125	143	161	179
29	18	36	54	72	87	103	121	138	156	173
30	17	34	51	67	84	100	117	134	150	167
31	17	33	49	65	81	97	113	139	146	162
32	16	32	47	63	79	94	110	126	141	167

PAPER USAGE GUIDE

Use the following chart as a general reference guide for determining which papers are most suitable for a given job.

Paper Type/ Standard Size (inches and cm)	Characteristics/ Colors	Finishes	Typical Sizes (inches)	Basis Weights (lb)	Primary Uses
Bond 17 × 22 (43.2 × 55.9 cm)	Comes in a range of pastels, neutrals, matching envelopes, and cover weights	Smooth, cockle	8½ × 11, 8½ × 14, 11 × 17, 17 × 22, 17 × 28, 19 × 24, 19 × 28, 23 × 35 rolls	16, 20, 24	Fliers, forms, photocopies, newsletters
Writing paper 17 × 22 (43.2 × 55.9 cm)	Comes in a range of colors and flocking options that match envelopes, plus cover and text weights	Smooth, linen laid, vellum, cockle, and more	8½ × 11, 17 × 22, 22½ × 35, 23 × 35, 25 × 38 rolls	24, 28	Stationery
Uncoated book 25 × 38 (63.5 × 96.5 cm)	Comes in a range of colors and is thicker and more opaque than bond or writing papers	Smooth	8½ × 11, 8½ × 14, 17½ × 22½, 23 × 29, 22½ × 35, 23 × 35, 25 × 38, 35 × 45, 38 × 50 rolls	30, 32, 35, 40, 45, 50, 60, 65, 70, 80	Books, direct mail, newsletters, catalogs
Text 25 × 38 (63.5 × 96.5 cm)	Comes in a range of colors and flocking options that match envelopes, plus cover and text weights	Smooth, linen laid, vellum, cockle, and more	8½ × 11, 17½ × 22½, 23 × 35, 25 × 38, 26 × 40	60, 65, 70, 75, 80, 100	Letterhead, annual reports, brochures, posters, brochures, direct mail, books
Coated book 25 × 38 (63.5 × 96.5 cm)	Matching cover weights limited to white and cream although specialty lines exist in a range of colors	Dull, gloss, matte, cast coated, some embossed finishes	19 × 25, 23 × 29, 23 × 35, 25 × 38, 35 × 45, 38 × 50	40, 45, 50, 60, 70, 80, 100	Magazines, catalogs, books, direct mail, annual reports
Cover 20 × 26 (50.8 × 66 cm)	Heavier and more durable counterpart to coordinate with text, book, and writing papers	Smooth, cockle, linen laid, vellum, dull, gloss, matte, cast coated	20 × 26, 23 × 35, 35 × 38, 26 × 40	60, 65, 80, 100, 120, 130	Business cards, covers for annual reports, brochures, menus, tickets, postcards, pocket folders, greeting cards
Index/Bristol 22½ × 28½ (57.2 × 72.4 cm)	Comes in a range of colors and finishes	Coated, vellum, smooth	22 × 28, 22½ × 28½, 23 × 35, 24 × 36, 25½ × 30½, 28 × 44	67, 90, 100, 110, 125, 140, 150, 175	Postcards, file folders, index cards, boxes, tickets, clothing tags
Translucent vellum	Semitransparent stock comes in a range of colors and weights plus matching envelopes	Smooth, grooved	8½ × 11, 23 × 35, 25 × 38	17, 21¼, 24, 27, 29, 40, 48, 53	Fly sheets, overlays, see-thru envelopes for invitations and other mailings
Newsprint 24 × 36 (61 × 91.5 cm)	Inexpensive, lightweight, white/ manila only	Vellum	Rolls	30	Newspapers, tabloids
Label	Comes in gummed, pressure sensitive, self-adhesive backing, and in a range of colors	Smooth (uncoated), matte, dull, glossy, and cast coated	8½ × 11, 17 × 22, 20 × 26, 24 × 30 rolls	60, 70	Labels, signs, stickers
Kraft 24 × 36 (61 × 91.5 cm)	Strong and durable, brown/ manila only	Vellum	Rolls	30, 40, 50	Bags, envelopes

STANDARD BINDING TYPES

There are many ways to bind loose sheets, folded sheets, or signatures together—each with its own set of aesthetic, cost, and durability considerations. Here is an overview of the binding options most readily available. Consult the chart following this section to compare the cost, durability, and aesthetic attributes of these binding methods.

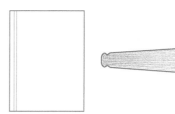

PERFECT BINDING

Signatures are gathered in a stack rather than nested. The spine side of the stack is milled to remove the folded edges. Melted adhesive is applied along the spine edges of the pages. The cover is applied while the glue is hot and wrapped around the book. The book is trimmed on a three-knife trimmer.

CASE BINDING (SMYTHE SEWN)

Gathered signatures are assembled and sewn along the spine. The sewn book block is then glued on the spine and trimmed on three sides. The trimmed book block is then glued to an outer cover, which is manufactured separately. The case is held to the book block by endsheets attached to the first and last signatures and glued to the inside.

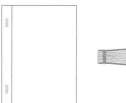

SADDLE STITCH BINDING

Cover and signatures are nested one within the other and hung over a chain or "saddle." Covers are scored and folded on the same machine and then laid on top of the signatures. Cover and signatures are wire stitched (stapled) at the center of the spine, and then trimmed.

SIDE STITCH BINDING

Cover and individual pages or signatures are collated and assembled into a stack and then wire stitched (stapled) at the bound edge.

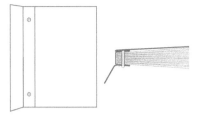

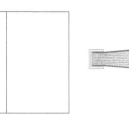

SCREW AND POST BINDING
Cover and signatures or individual pages are collated and assembled in a stack and trimmed on all sides, then drilled and fastened together with posts held on by screws. Screws can be unscrewed to add or remove pages as needed.

TAPE BINDING
Signatures and covers are assembled, collated, and trimmed on all sides. A strip of flexible cloth tape that contains glue is applied on the edges of the spine and heated. The glue melts and spreads, gluing the covers and signatures together.

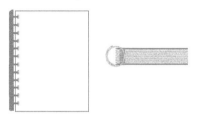

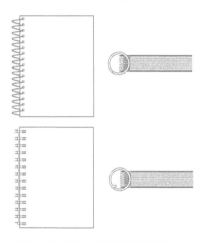

PLASTIC COMB BINDING
Trimmed covers and individual pages are assembled, collated, and held together by a plastic comb that is opened, inserted into drilled holes, and then closed. Comb can be opened to insert more pages as needed.

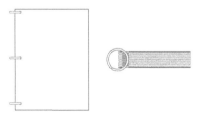

SPIRAL AND DOUBLE-LOOP WIRE BINDING
Trimmed covers and individual pages are assembled, collated, and held together by a spiraled piece of plastic, wire, or doubled wire inserted into drilled holes.

RING BINDING
Trimmed covers and individual pages are assembled, collated, and held together by individual rings. Or individual pages are assembled, collated, and inserted into a binder with rings. Rings and binders come in a variety of sizes and colors. Pages can be added or subtracted as needed.

WHICH BINDING METHOD WORKS BEST?

Bindings differ in their appearance, cost, and function. Some binding styles are suitable for publications with many pages, whereas others will only work for those with a limited number of pages. Some methods allow pages to lie flat, whereas others don't. Durability and cost are other considerations. Saddle stitching, for instance, is relatively inexpensive but not as permanent as case binding. The following chart should give you a better idea of which options will best suit your publication's design and budget.

Binding Style	Girth	Lays Flat	Printable Spine	Durability	Relative Cost	Advantages	Limitations
Case	3" for hardcover, 1³⁄₄" for paperback	Yes	Yes	High	High	Strength, durability, and a look of quality.	Most costly option. Requires more production time. Requires signatures.
Perfect	Up to 2³⁄₈"	No	Yes, for ¹⁄₈" and larger	Moderate	Low	Inexpensive for moderate runs of of 1,000–5,000. Can bind single sheets.	Paper grain must run parallel to the binding edge. Image area may be lost in gutter.
Saddle Stitch	Up to ¹⁄₂"	Yes	No	Moderate	Low	Fast and inexpensive. Can easily accomodate inserts.	Requires signatures. Pages must be in increments of four. May need adjustments for creep.
Side Stitch	Up to 1"	No	No	High	Low	Fast and inexpensive. Variety of wire styles and widths available.	Pages won't lie flat when open. Requires a minimum 1" margin.
Screw and Post	Up to 1"	No	No	High	High	Easy to insert additional pages. Can accommodate pages of different materials.	Hand assembly is time consuming and not appropriate for large quantities.
Tape	Up to 1³⁄₄"	Yes	No	Moderate	High	Durable option that is less costly than case binding. Tape comes in a range of colors.	Requires signatures. Pages must be in increments of four.
Plastic Comb	Up to 1³⁄₄"	Yes	Possible with foil stamping	Low	Low for small runs	Widely available. Can be reopened to insert other pages. Facing pages align.	Time consuming and costly for large quantities.
Spiral	Up to 2" and folds over 360°	Yes	No	Moderate	Moderate	Well suited to short runs. Can accommodate pages of different materials.	Because of jogging, crossover designs may not align.
Ring	Up to 3"	Yes	Binders can be screen printed	Low	Cost of materials for in-house hand assembly	Easy to insert additional pages. Can accommodate pages of different materials.	Hand assembly is inappropriate for large runs, but good for custom applications.

FOLD BASICS

Basic valley and mountain folds are used to create a series of peaks and troughs, which make up all common fold styles.

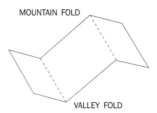

MOUNTAIN FOLD

VALLEY FOLD

COMMON FOLD STYLES

Fold styles have standard names that should be used when communicating with printers and binderies. Following is a list of some of the most common styles and their names.

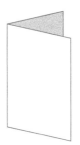

FOUR-PAGE SIMPLE FOLD

One fold made along either the short or long dimension of the paper resulting in four panels or pages.

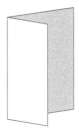

FOUR-PAGE SHORT FOLD

A simple fold made asymmetrically so that two pages or panels are larger than the others.

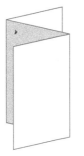

SIX-PAGE ACCORDION FOLD OR Z-FOLD

Two simple folds where one fold bends in the opposite direction of the other resulting in six panels or pages. Accordion folds can comprise six, eight, ten, and sometimes twelve panels or pages.

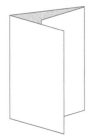

SIX-PAGE BARREL OR ROLL FOLD

Two simple folds where the outer edges of each panel or page are folded in toward the other resulting in six panels or pages. Barrel or roll folds composed of more than six panels or pages are often called rolling folds and can consist of many panels or pages.

Heavy text and cover stock needs to be scored before it's folded, preferably in the direction of the grain. Folding against the grain, even with a score, may result in problems. To determine the grain direction of your sheet, fold it vertically and then horizontally. When it's folded with the grain, the fold line will be much more even than when it's folded against the grain.

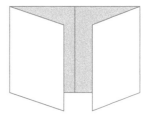

EIGHT-PAGE GATEFOLD
A barrel fold with an additional fold in the center, resulting in eight panels or pages.

EIGHT-PAGE FRENCH FOLD/SIXTEEN-PAGE SIGNATURE
Multiple fold where the paper is first folded in one direction, then folded perpendicular to the first fold. This configuration is also used when creating sixteen-page signatures.

EIGHT-PAGE PARALLEL FOLD
A combination of a barrel fold and an accordion fold that forms eight panels or pages.

TOLERANCES FOR GATEFOLDS, BARREL, OR ROLL FOLDS

Gatefolds, as well as barrel or roll folds, require special allowances so that the outer panels or pages of a piece will overlap those within. Although the following standards apply to text weight papers, tolerances may vary slightly with other types of paper.

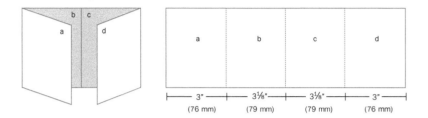

Gatefolds require an additional ⅛ inch (3.175 mm) on the outer panels (b and c) in the fold sequence.

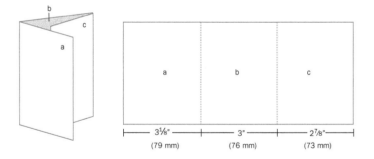

Roll or barrel folds require an additional ⅛ inch (3.175 mm) for each panel in the fold sequence so that each panel is ⅛ inch (3.175 mm) larger than the next.

○ Chapter 9: Envelopes and Folders

ENVELOPE CONSTRUCTION

This diagram shows the basic parts of an envelope. Refer to these terms when working with envelope converters or others involved in envelope printing and manufacturing.

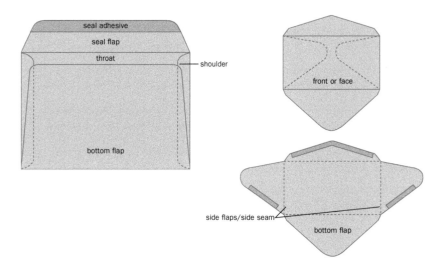

CLOSURE DESIGNATION

Closure designation is described by the location of the envelope opening and seal flap. Aesthetic and functional considerations should guide your decision on which of the following types to select.

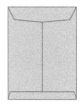

OPEN END (OE)

The opening and seal flap are located on the short dimension. Open-end envelopes are well suited to hand-insertion applications.

OPEN SIDE (OS)

The opening and seal flap are located on the long dimension. Open-side envelopes are well suited to automatic as well as hand-insertion applications.

STANDARD ENVELOPE STYLES AND SIZES

Envelopes come in a variety of styles that vary according to function. Some styles are more suitable for invitations and announcements, while others are appropriate for business use. Each style is available in a range of standard sizes. Consult the diagrams and listings below to determine which style and type of envelope is best for your job.

COMMERCIAL AND OFFICIAL (UNITED STATES)

Standard correspondence-style envelopes. Open-sided with gummed flaps. Made in a wide range of bond and kraft. Commercial sizes range from no. 5 to no. 6¾. Official sizes range from no. 7 to no. 14.

BOOKLET (UNITED STATES)

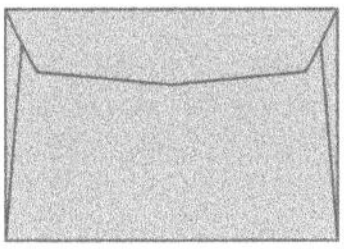

For use with booklets, folders, and other types of direct mail. Open-side design permits overall printing.

Item/No.	Size (inches)	Size (centimeters)
5	3¹⁄₁₆ × 5½	7.78 × 13.97
6	3⅜ × 6	8.5725 × 15.24
6¼	3½ × 6	8.89 × 15.24
6½	3⁹⁄₁₆ × 6½	9.05 × 16.51
6¾	3⅝ × 6½	9.2075 × 16.51
7	3¾ × 6¾	9.525 × 16.145
7½	3¾ × 7⅝	9.525 × 19.3675
7¾ (Monarch)	3⅞ × 7½	9.8425 × 19.05
Data Card	3½ × 7⅝	8.89 × 19.3675
8⅝ (Check)	3⅝ × 8⅝	9.2075 × 21.9075
9	3⅞ × 8⅞	9.8425 × 22.5425
10	4⅛ × 9½	10.4775 × 24.13
10½	4½ × 9½	11.43 × 24.13
11	4½ × 10⅜	11.43 × 26.3525
12	4¾ × 11	12.065 × 27.94
14	5 × 11½	12.7 × 29.21

Item/No.	Size (inches)	Size (centimeters)
2½	4½ × 5⅞	11.43 × 14.9225
3	4¾ × 6½	12.065 × 16.51
4¼	5 × 7½	12.7 × 19.05
5	5½ × 8½	13.97 × 21.59
6	5¾ × 8⅞	14.605 × 22.5425
6½	6 × 9	15.24 × 22.86
6¾	6½ × 9½	16.51 × 24.13
7	6¼ × 9⅝	15.875 × 24.44475
7¼	7 × 10	17.78 × 25.4
7½	7½ × 10½	19.05 × 26.67
8	8 × 11⅛	20.32 × 28.2575
9	8¾ × 11½	22.225 × 29.21
9½	9 × 12	22.86 × 30.48
10	9½ × 12⅝	24.13 × 32.0675
13	10 × 13	25.4 × 33.02

TICKET (UNITED STATES)

Open-side envelope for theater tickets. Often printed with advertising.

Item/No.	Size (inches)	Size (centimeters)
3	1⁵⁄₁₆ × 4 ⁷⁄₁₆	3.3350 × 11.2725

WINDOW (UNITED STATES)

Permit name and address typed on the enclosure to show through the window. Used for invoices, statements, checks, receipts, etc.

WINDOW (UNITED STATES)

Item/No.	Size (inches)	Size (centimeters)
6¼	3½ × 6	8.89 × 15.24
6¾	3⅝ × 6½	9.2075 × 16.51
7	3¾ × 6¾	9.525 × 16.145
7¾	3⅞ × 7½	9.8425 × 19.05
8⅝	3⅝ × 8⅞	9.2075 × 21.9075
9	3⅞ × 8⅞	9.8425 × 22.5425
10	4⅛ × 9½	10.4775 × 24.13
11	4½ × 10⅜	11.43 × 26.3525
12	4¾ × 11	12.065 × 27.94
14	5 × 11½	12.7 × 29.21

WINDOW SIZE AND POSITION (UNITED STATES)

Window size 4¾ × 1⅛ inches (120.65 × 28.5 mm). Position ⅞ inch (22.2 mm) from left, ⅝ inch (15.87 mm) from bottom. Size 8⅝ inches (219.0 mm) is ⅝ inch (15.87 mm) from left, ¹³⁄₁₆ inches (20.6 mm) from bottom.

WINDOW (CANADA)

Item/No.	Size (inches)	Size (millimeters)
8	3⅝ × 6½	92.075 × 165.1
Banker's Check	3⅝ × 7⅞	92.075 × 200.025
Check	3⅝ × 8⅝	92.075 × 219.075
No. 8½	3¾ × 6¾	95.25 × 161.45
Large Check	3¾ × 8¾	95.25 × 222.25
Tu Fold	4 × 7½	101.6 × 190.5
No. 9	4 × 9	101.6 × 228.6
T-4	4⅛ × 9	104.775 × 228.6
No. 10	4⅛ × 9½	104.775 × 241.3
Broker Window	4⅛ × 9½	104.775 × 241.3
No. 11	4½ × 9⅝	114.3 × 244.475

REMITTANCE (UNITED STATES)

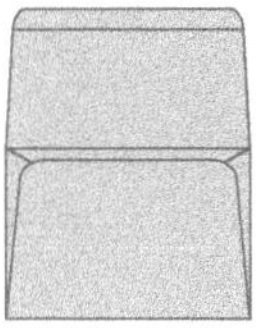

CATALOG (UNITED STATES)

Large flap can be printed to contain any message. Used for coupons, credit information, applications, statements, etc.

Item/No.	Size (inches)	Size (centimeters)
6¼	3½ × 6 (3⅜ flap)	8.89 × 15.24 (7.9375 flap)
6½	3½ × 6¼ (3⅜ flap)	8.89 × 15.5575 (8.5725 flap)
6¾	3⅝ × 6½ (3½ flap)	9.2075 × 16.51 (8.89 flap)
9	3⅞ × 8⅞	9.8425 × 22.5425

Open-end style. Wide seams with heavy gummed flaps provide good protection for mail handling of catalogs, magazines, reports, etc.

Item/No.	Size (inches)	Size (millimeters)
1	6 × 9	152.4 × 228.6
1¾	6½ × 9½	165.1 × 241.3
2	6 ½ × 10	165.1 × 254
3	7 × 10	177.8 × 254
6	7½ × 10½	190.5 × 266.7
7	8 × 11	203.2 × 279.4
8	8¼ × 11¼	209.55 × 285.75
9½	8½ × 10½	215.9 × 266.7
9¾	8¾ × 11¼	222.25 × 285.75
10½	9 × 12	228.6 × 304.8
12½	9 ½ × 12½	241.3 × 317.5
13½	10 × 13	254 × 330.2
14¼	11¼ × 14¼	285.75 × 361.95
14½	11½ × 14½	292.1 × 368.3

POLICY (UNITED STATES)

Primarily used for insurance policies. Also used to hold bonds, mortgages, and other legal papers.

Item/No.	Size (inches)	Size (millimeters)
9	4 × 9	101.6 × 228.6
10	4⅛ × 9½	104.775 × 241.3
11	4½ × 10⅜	114.3 × 263.25
12	4¾ × 10⅞	276.225 × 276.2
14	5 × 11½	127 × 292.1

METAL CLASP (UNITED STATES)

Strong and durable. Ideal for mailing bulky papers and heavy publications. Can be opened and closed many times.

Item/No.	Size (inches)	Size (millimeters)
0	2½ × 4 × ¼	63.5 × 104.775
5	3⅛ × 5½	79.375 × 139.7
10	3⅜ × 6	85.725 × 152.4
11	4½ × 10⅜	114.3 × 263.525
14	5 × 11½	127 × 292.1
15	4 × 6 ³/₈	101.6 × 161.925
25	4⅝ × 6 ¾	117.474 × 171.45
35	5 × 7½	127 × 190.5
50	5½ × 8¼	139.7 × 209.55
55	6 × 9	152.4 × 228.6
63	6½ × 9½	165.1 × 241.3
68	7 × 10	177.8 × 254
75	7½ × 10	190.5 × 254
80	8 × 11	203.2 × 279.4
83	8½ × 11½	215.9 × 292.1
87	8¾ × 11¼	222.25 × 285.75
90	9 × 12	228.6 × 304.8
93	9½ × 12½	241.3 × 317.5
94	9¼ × 14½	234.95 × 368.3
95	10 × 12	254 × 304.8
97	10 × 13	254 × 330.2
98	10 × 15	254 × 381
105	11½ × 14½	279.4 × 368.3
110	12 × 15½	304.8 × 393.7

ANNOUNCEMENT OR A-STYLE

Made for use with a wide range of matching text and cover papers. May also have deckle (ragged cut) edge and flaps.

Item/No.	Size (inches)	Size (millimeters)
A-2	4⅜ × 5¾	111.125 × 146.05
A-6	4¾ × 6½	120.65 × 165.1
A-7	5¼ × 7¼	133.35 × 184.15
A-8	5½ × 8⅛	139.7 × 206.375
A-10	6 × 9½	152.4 × 241.3
A-Long	3⅞ × 8⅞	98.425 × 225.425

WALLET FLAP

Mostly used by banks or investment firms for mailing statements and other documents. Deep flap and extra wide gummed area offer protection to the contents.

Item/No.	Size (inches)	Size (millimeters)
10	4⅛ × 9½	104.775 × 241.3
11	4½ × 10⅜	114.3 × 263.525
12	4¾ × 11	120.65 × 279.4
14	5 × 11½	127 × 292.1
16	6 × 12	1524 × 304.8

BUSINESS ANNOUNCEMENT AND BARONIAL

Formal envelopes with deep, pointed flaps. Widely used for invitations, formal announcements, greeting, and social cards.

Item/No.	Size (inches)	Size (millimeters)
Gladstone	3⁹⁄₁₆ × 5⁹⁄₁₆	90.500 × 141.300
4 Baronial	3⅝ × 5⅛	92.075 × 130.175
5 Baronial	4⅛ × 5⅛	104.775 × 130.175
5¼ Baronial	4¼ × 5¼	107.95 × 133.35
53	4⅛ × 6¼	104.775 × 158.75
5½ Baronial	4⅜ × 5⅝	111.125 × 142.875
6 Baronial	5 × 6¼	127 × 158.75
110	5 × 7¼	127 × 180.975
Lee	5¼ × 7¼	133.35 × 184.15
137	5½ × 8½	139.7 × 215.9

COIN

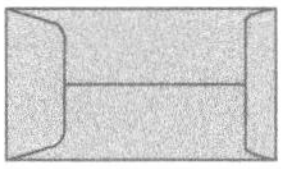

Used for paper currency as well as coins by banks and corporations.

Item/No.	Size (inches)	Size (millimeters)
00	1¹¹⁄₁₆ × 2¾	42.875 × 69.85
1	2¼ × 3½	57.15 × 88.9
3	2½ × 4¼	63.5 × 107.95
4	3 × 4½	76.2 × 114.3
5	2⅞ × 5¼	73.025 × 133.35
5½	3¼ × 5½	88.9 × 139.7
6	3⅜ × 6	85.725 × 152.4
7	3½ × 6½	88.9 × 165.1

INTERNATIONAL ENVELOPE SIZES

International, or ISO, envelope sizes are based on folding A4 (210 × 297 mm, letterhead sized) paper into an envelope. Other sizes and how they fit when folded into the various ISO envelope sizes are shown below.

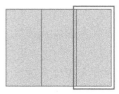

An A4 folded twice into thirds fits in a DL envelope.

An A4 folded once fits in a C5 envelope.

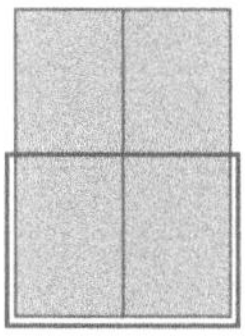

An A5 folded once fits in a C6 envelope.

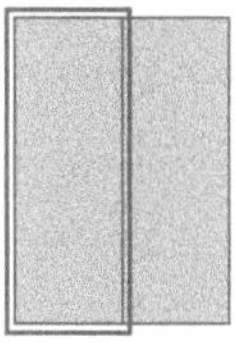

An A5 folded once fits in a DL envelope.

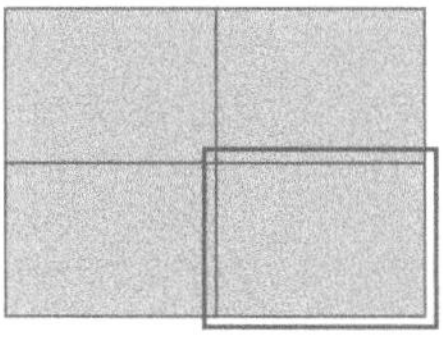

An A4 folded twice into quarters fits in a C6 envelope.

PRINTING CONSIDERATIONS FOR ENVELOPES

· *Paper mills and commercial printers rely on envelope converters to cut, fold, glue, and assemble envelopes. Envelopes are either premade by an envelope converter and sold by paper distributors as a product made from a mill's writing and text papers, or they are custom made by envelope converters from paper after it has been printed. Premade envelopes are less expensive than converting from flat sheets.*

· *Envelopes printed in four color, printed on the inside or covered entirely with exterior graphics need to be printed before they are converted into envelopes.*

· *Embossing or engraving will show through on the opposite side of a premade envelope, unless the tecnique is confined to the envelope flap.*
It is best to engrave or emboss before the envelope is converted.

· *Printing, engraving, or embossing envelopes before conversion is more expensive and time consuming and not appropriate for small runs. However, if you plan to produce a quantity of 5,000 or more, printing before conversion may be within your budget. Anticipate at least three weeks for envelope conversion and check with your vendor to find out exactly what the time frame will be.*

· *When printing on premade envelopes, confine graphics and return address information to the upper-left corner of the envelope. Postal regulations require that the face of the envelope be left blank for address and postal information. A $\frac{3}{8}$-inch (9.525 mm) allowance also needs to be made at the envelope's edges to accommodate press grippers.*

Consult the following chart for standard ISO envelope sizes:

Size	In millimeters	Approximate inches
C3	324 × 458	12.76 × 18.03
B4	250 × 353	9.84 × 13.89
C4	229 × 324	9.01 × 12.76
B5	176 × 250	6.93 × 9.84
C5	162 × 229	6.38 × 9.01
B6/C4	125 × 324	4.92 × 12.75
B6	125 × 176	4.92 × 6.92
C6	114 × 162	4.49 × 6.38
DL	110 × 220	4.33 × 8.66
C7/C6	81 × 162	3.19 × 6.38
C7	81 × 114	3.19 × 4.49

POCKET FOLDER STYLES

This two-pocket folder with glued flaps is an economical choice suitable for lightweight inserts, such as sample sheets or small brochures. It can be easily adapted to a one pocket configuration by eliminating one of the flaps. The business card slot can also be deleted if it isn't necessary. *For template see page 94*

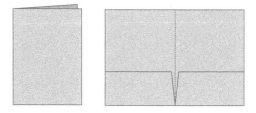

This three-pocket configuration folds to the same 9" × 12" (228.6 x 304.8 mm) size as the two-pocket configuration but opens to reveal an additional pocket. The folder features glued flaps at either end and an unglued flap on the center panel. *For template see page 95*

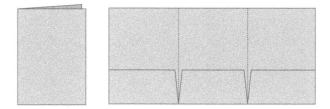

Square flaps can accommodate more inserts and bulkier documents than standard pocket folders. They work especially well for magazine media kits. Be sure to use heavy or laminated cover stock to achieve the necessary rigidity. *For template see page 96*

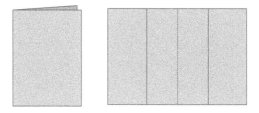

The following pocket folder templates are printed at ¼ scale. Enlarge them by 400% when scanning to bring them up to their actual size.

Template: Standard Two-Pocket Folder

Template: Three-Pocket Folder

Template: Two-Pocket Folder with Box Side Flaps

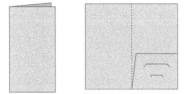

This single-pocket folder has slots to hold two types of room keys. It folds to fit in a jacket pocket or purse.

Template: Single-Pocket Room Key Folder

Pocket folders offer a means of containing materials that will immediately add polish and professionalism to a presentation. However, they present some unique planning and production challenges.

· Pick a folder style and size that is suitable for your inserts. It's common to plan a folder with more or larger pockets than necessary with the assumption that too much space is better than not enough. However, pockets that are too large for their inserts will allow folder materials to move around, resulting in a messy presentation.

· For a sturdy folder, select a cover stock with a basis weight that is between 100 and 120 lb. (270 gsm and 325 gsm). Have a paper dummy made to determine if the stock you've chosen for your pocket folder will be suitable for the inserts.

· Box pocket folders and those with three panels often require hand assembly, a factor that will add time and expense to your job. Take this into consideration when determining the size and style of a folder.

· Most commercial printers have dies for pocket folders on hand, or use a vendor with a selection from which to choose. To save time and money, check to find out what size and pocket configurations are available before you start to design.

TRAY-STYLE CARTONS

A basic type of folding carton is the tray, a relatively shallow carton with a bottom hinged to a wide side and end walls. The sides and ends are connected by a flap, hook, locking tab, or lock that can be glued or assembled without glue. Tray cartons can also consist of two pieces, one slightly larger than the other, forming the base and cover of a two-piece telescoping box. Trays are often used for baked goods, cigarettes, for food service items, and as pizza carryout containers.

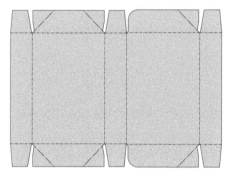

Six-Point Glued Tray with Integral Lid

Preglued corners provide extra strength and ease of assembly. Structure is erected by pulling out the sides of the tray. Because it stores flat and is easily opened, this type of container works well in the fast-food industry.

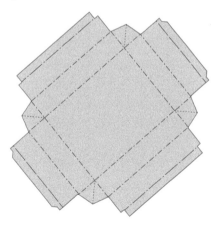

Web Corner Tray

Easy-erect tray cartons assemble without glue. The diagonal fold across each corner creates a web that's held in place by flaps. An appropriate alternative in situations when gluing isn't an option.

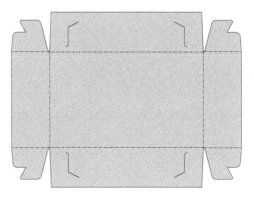

Corner-Locked Tray

Another option when gluing isn't available is tongue-and-slot corners that are used to form sides. This option is not as rigid as the web corner tray, however, it uses less material. This style can be made into a container with a lid by using one tray as the base and a slightly larger one for the lid.

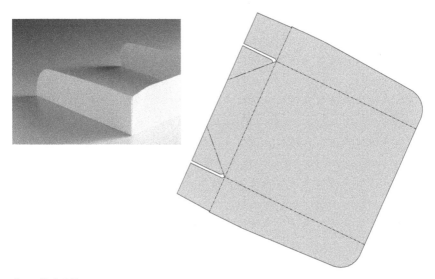

Open-Ended Tray

Glue-assembled trays are frequently used for baked goods and other food items when display of product is important. Product is protected with shrink-wrap, cellophane, or other transparent wrapping.

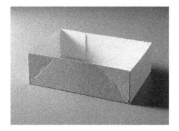
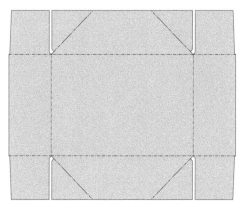

In-Fold/Out-Fold Tray

Glue-cornered trays store flat and then self-erect when the sides are lifted. They can be shrink-wrapped when display of product is important. They can also be formed into a container with a lid by using one tray as the base and a slightly larger one for the lid in a combination often used for gift boxes.

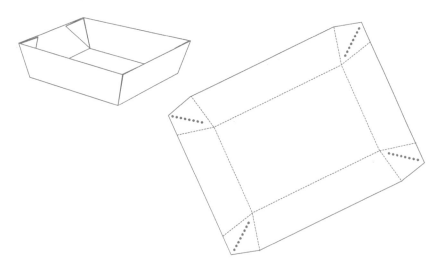

Glue-Cornered Taper Tray

Preassembled and glued trays stack well and can function equally well as a plate or dish. they are frequently used in the food service industry for serving french fries, salads, and other nonliquid products.

BASIC TUBE-STYLE CARTONS

Tube-style folding cartons are rectangular sleeves formed from a sheet of board that is folded over and glued against its edges. Tubes have openings at the top and bottom that are closed with flaps, reverse, or straight tucks and locks that can be glued or assembled without glue.

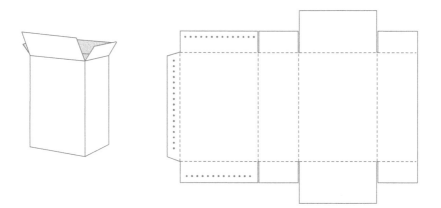

Skillet or Sealed End Carton

Flaps are sealed using glue or tape. Most shipping cartons use this configuration and closure because it provides the most economical use of carton board.

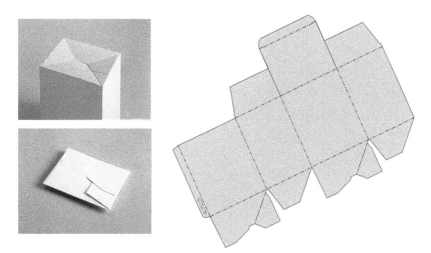

Tuck-Top Crash Base Carton

Used when fast assembly of the carton is important. Cartons are preglued and folded flat. When opened for assembly, the base slides into position and locks when all sides meet.

BASIC CLOSURE TYPES

In addition to providing a temporary barrier between the package's contents and the outside, the closure can also contribute to the rigidity of the carton. The closure may also determine or transform the purpose of a carton.

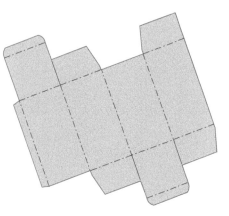

Standard Tuck-Flap

Appropriate for individually wrapped items such as bandages or products in squeezable tubes. Also a good choice as a container for food items such as tea and sugar packets where reusability is important. May require a seal or outer wrapping to ensure contents will remain intact prior to purchase.

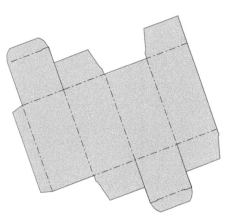

Slit-Lock Tuck

Applications are similar to standard tuck-flap carton, except slits provide a more secure seal. For tamper resistance, add a seal or a protective outer wrapping.

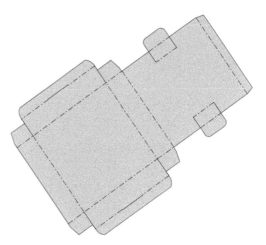

Tab Lock
Slits and tab provide additional protection against tampering and lid being forced open by inside pressure from the contents.

Postal Lock
Although not reusable, this completely tamperproof option has an arrowhead tab that tears on opening, providing proof of entry.

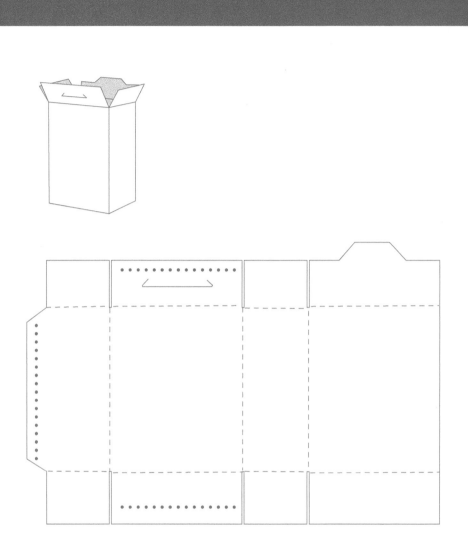

Partial Overlap Seal End with Lock Tab and Lock Slot
This closure option is appropriate for items contained in an interior, moistureproof pouch including cereal, cookies, or crackers. The top is often glued shut to prevent tampering prior to purchase, leaving the tab and slot as a reusable closure after the carton is opened.

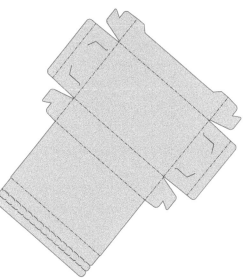

Pull-Strip or Zipper Carton
Commonly used to prevent tampering. The pull-strip provides an irreversible method of opening. Suitable for cereals, crackers, and other foods contained in an interior, moisture-proof pouch. Note: All flaps must be glued or have locking closures to prevent access via another entrance and to ensure pull-strip will be properly aligned.

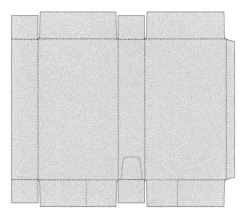

Pour-Spout Container
Score lines along the container's top and side allow the consumer to access the product and pour the contents in a controlled manner. This type of carton is commonly used for cereal and detergent.

FOLDERS, SLEEVES, AND OTHER TYPES OF FOLDING CARTONS

These packaging options suit the needs of specialty packaging and specific products.

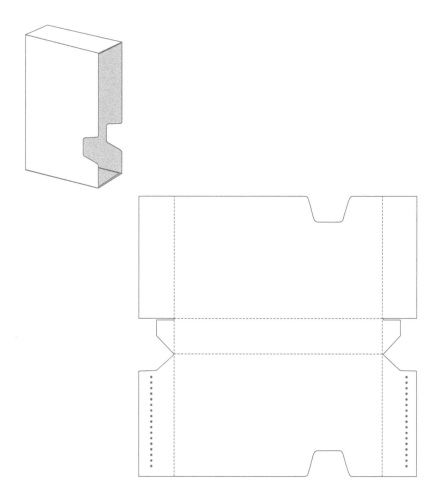

Open-End Sleeve with Finger Holes

Finger holes and open-end construction allow easy access to the object inside the sleeve.

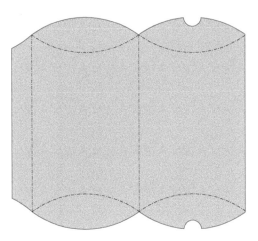

Pillow Pack

Functions well for packaging soft items such as clothing or a number of small pieces. Easily assembled and can be stored in flat-packed state. Package design can also be easily modified to a pull-strip closure.

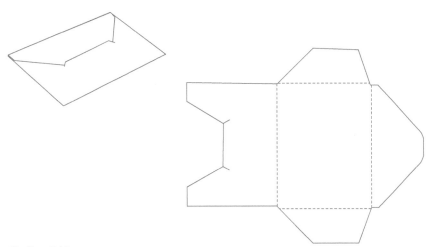

Shallow Folder

This type of package makes economical use of resources for packaging flat items such as hosiery. Its tuck-in closure can be sealed or replaced with a pull-strip to make the container tamper resistant.

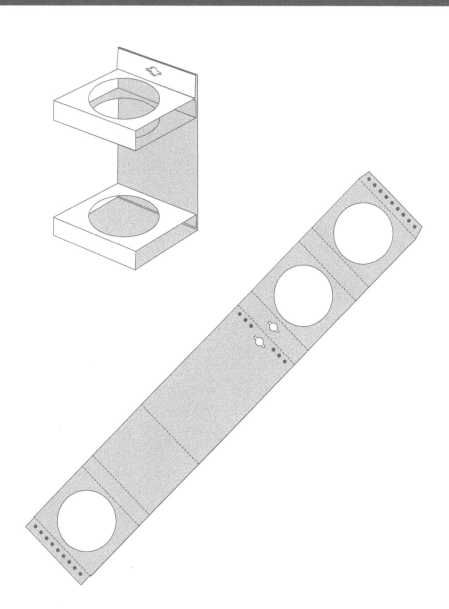

Bottle Hanger

This one-piece construction lends itself to a variety of lightweight, cylindrical items and provides maximum product visibility.

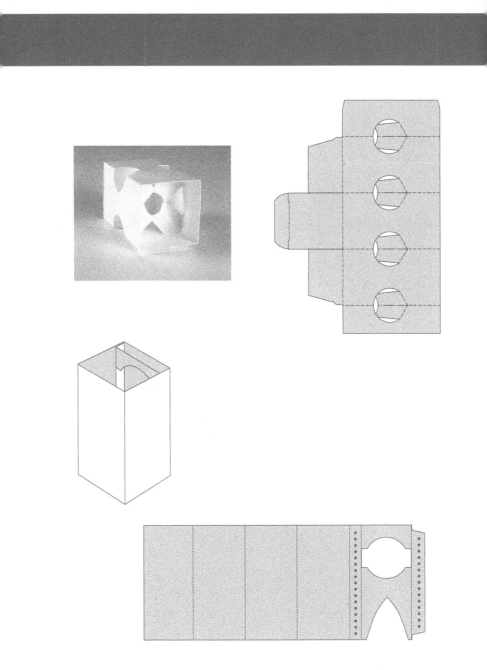

Lightbulb Sleeve

These designs use inner panels and die cuts to protect and immobilize lightbulbs.
The design can be modified to suit similarly fragile products.

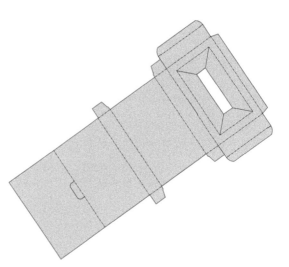

Display Carton
The extended lid flap on this carton opens to reveal a display recess to accommodate a product. Cut from a single sheet, this design requires only one side of the board to be printed.

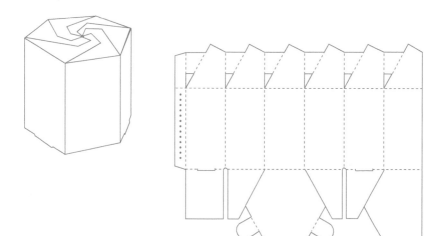

Six-Sided Carton with Push-In Closure
The small triangles have been die-cut out of the top closure to permit easier closing. Assembly requires glue on the side but not on the bottom of the carton. Suitable for novelty and gift items.

SET-UP BOXES

Set-up or rigid paper boxes are assembled by piecing together flat sheets of boxboard, which are held together at the sides with corner stays and adhesive. The assembled box is covered with decorative paper that is adhered to the exterior surface. Unlike folding cartons, which are often delivered flat, set-up boxes are delivered as a three-dimensional product ready to be filled with merchandise. They can be easily adapted to a variety of applications that may include platforms, plastic domes, or compartments. Their decorative quality makes them suitable for cosmetics, candy, and jewelry. Set-up boxes instantly add an upscale look to gifts, gift boxes, and luxury items.

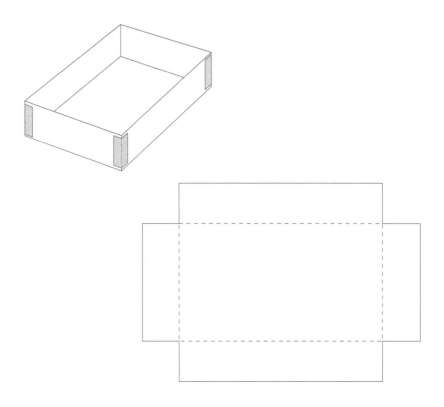

Basic Set-up Construction

A simple set-up box involves scoring a sheet of box board so that the sides can be folded at right angles to the base. The side panels are fastened at the corners with tape, fabric, or metal. The assembled box is covered with a precut sheet of paper that is scored at the fold lines, adhered to the outside, and wrapped around the box edges so that it covers a portion of the interior. Two trays, such as the one shown here, are typically combined to form a box and lid.

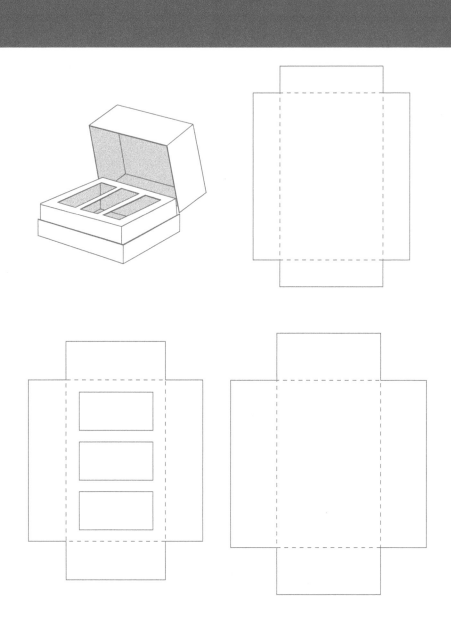

Lidded Box with Raised Platform

Boxes with raised platforms work well as a means of showcasing watches, jewelry, or other valuables. The platform openings can be replaced with slits for displaying rings or adapted in other ways, depending on the shape of the objects inside.

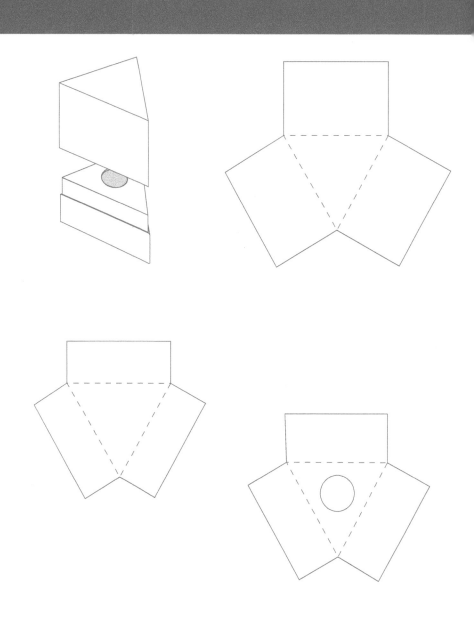

Triangular Box with Raised Platform

This alternative to the standard, four-sided box makes an unusual presentation. The deep lid makes this construction suitable for a perfume bottle or other vertical container.

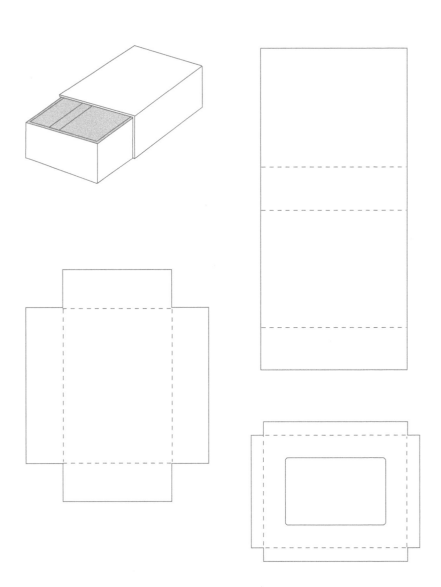

Tube and Slide

Without the platform, the tube and slide construction functions much like a matchbox as a container for loose items.

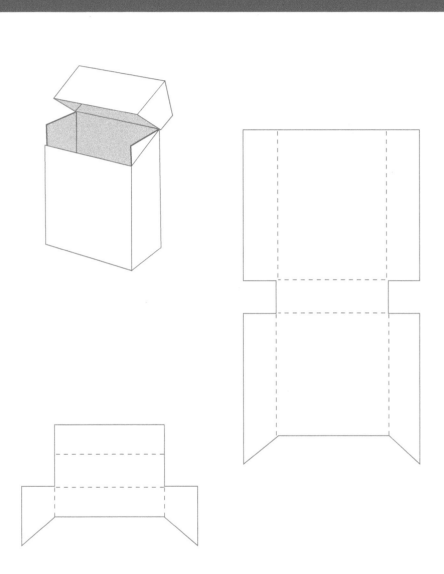

Hinged-Lid Box
The vertical nature of this box makes it an ideal container for chalk, crayons, discs, or as a document holder.

COMMON STYLES OF STOCK PLASTIC CONTAINERS

Plastic containers are generally categorized according to shape: oblong, oval, round, or square. From there, shapes vary according to function. Consult the following diagrams for an overview of some common shapes. Check with specific manufacturers for more specific information on capacity range, container materials, and barrier capabilities.

Classic Oblong

Vanity Oblong

Sprayer: Oblong

Angle Neck Oblong

Lexington Round

Regular Cylinder

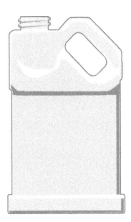

Handleware: Slant

Handleware: 2-Gal. Oblong

Sprayer: Pistol Grip

Wide-Mouth Oblong

Straight-Sided Oval

Tapered Oval

Syrup Oval

Boston Round

Bullet Round

Wide-Mouth Square

Carafe: Modern

Handleware: 1-Gal. (3.79 L) Round

Jar: Wide-Mouth Round

PAPER BAGS

Paper bags are constructed from a continuous web of paper that is formed into a tube and glued along the overlap to form a seam. The tube is torn to a specified length, frequently against a serrated bar, which gives the bag a saw-toothed edge. The end is folded over and glued to form the bottom. There are three general styles of bag construction: flat, square or pinch bottom, and automatic bottom or self-opening style (SOS).

Flat bags are inexpensive to produce and make economical use of materials. They work well for containing flat items such as cookies or greeting cards.

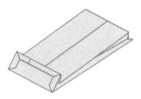

Square or pinch bottom bags can accommodate bulkier items and work well as shopping bags for single purchases of garments and other lightweight merchandise.

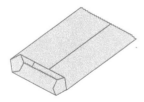

Automatic bottom or self-opening style bags are constructed with a more rigid bottom and are often made of kraft paper to serve as grocery bags or with attached handles to serve as shopping bags.

Other styles of bag construction include sewn open-mouth (left) and satchel (right).

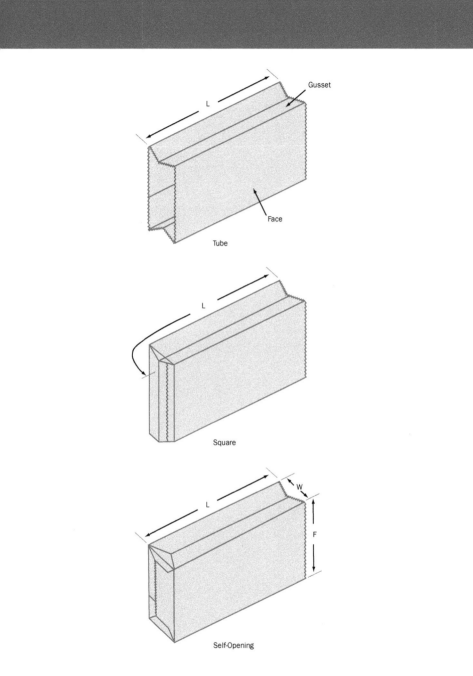

Tube

Square

Self-Opening

When planning bag construction, dimensions should be specified as face, width (or gusset), and length. Note that length is measured differently for a square (pinch bottom) bag and for a self-opening bag. The length of the tube before it is formed into a bag is sometimes given, and this should not be confused with the finished length (the finishing process reduces the tube length).

PLASTIC BAGS

Plastic bags are manufactured from plastic tubing or from a flat web that is folded and joined at a back seam. The ends are generally heat sealed to complete the closure.

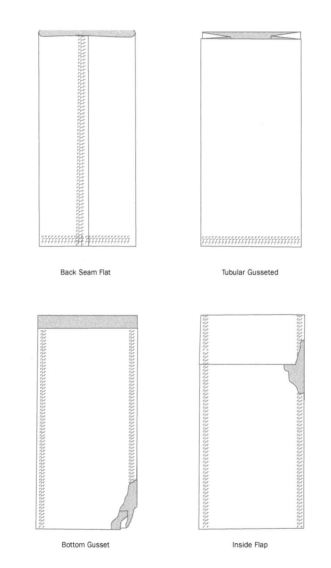

Back Seam Flat

Tubular Gusseted

Bottom Gusset

Inside Flap

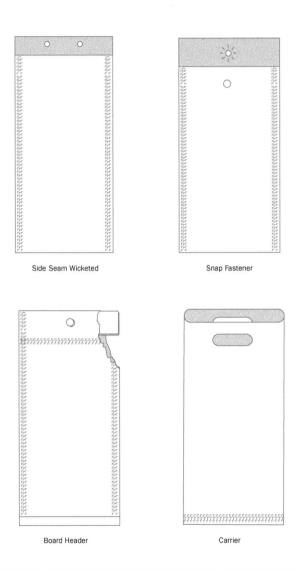

Side Seam Wicketed

Snap Fastener

Board Header

Carrier

Plastic bags can be manufactured as flat or gusseted and include a variety of styles and closures.

○ Chapter 11: Postal Standards

GENERAL USPS MAIL CLASSIFICATIONS AND REQUIREMENTS

The United States Postal Service (USPS) rates are based on mail that is automation compatible.

Machinable: mail pieces that fall within the min/max size specs, rectangular in shape, constructed of paper and sealed per USPS specifications. Charged at a lower rate.

Non-machinable: mail pieces that include rolls, tubes, and anything irregularly shaped, which do not comply with the size and aspect ration requirement and thus cannot be sorted on automated equipment. Charged at a higher rate.

Always show a folded mock-up to your post office agent to ensure it meets the USPS guidelines prior to finalizing your design. The standards and requirements listed are current at the time of publication. Visit www.usps.com for standards and requirements updates.

Postcard
Rectangular card stock mail piece not contained within an envelope.

Large envelope or flat
Flat, rectangular mail piece.

Letter
Small, rectangular mail piece.

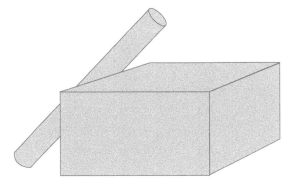

Package

A three-dimensional mail piece contained in a box, thick envelope, or tube.

Type	Height	Width	Thickness	Weight
Postcard	Min 3 ½ inches (89 mm); Max 4 ¼ inches (108 mm)	Min 5 inches (127mm); Max 6 inches (152 mm)	Min .007 inches (.178 mm); Max .016 inches inch (.406 mm)	n/a
Letter	Min 3 ½ inches (89 mm); Max 6 1/8 inches (156 mm)	Min 5 inches (127mm); Max 11 ½ inches (292 mm)	Min .007 inches (.178 mm); Max ¼ inch (6 mm)	Max 3.3 oz (94 g)
Large envelope or flat	Min 6 1/8 inches (155 mm); Max 12 inches (305 mm)	Min 11 ½ inches (295 mm); Max 15 ¾ inches (400mm)	Min ¼ inch (6 mm); Max ¾ inch (19 mm)	Max 13 oz (369 g) for first class; Max 16 oz (454 g) for standard class

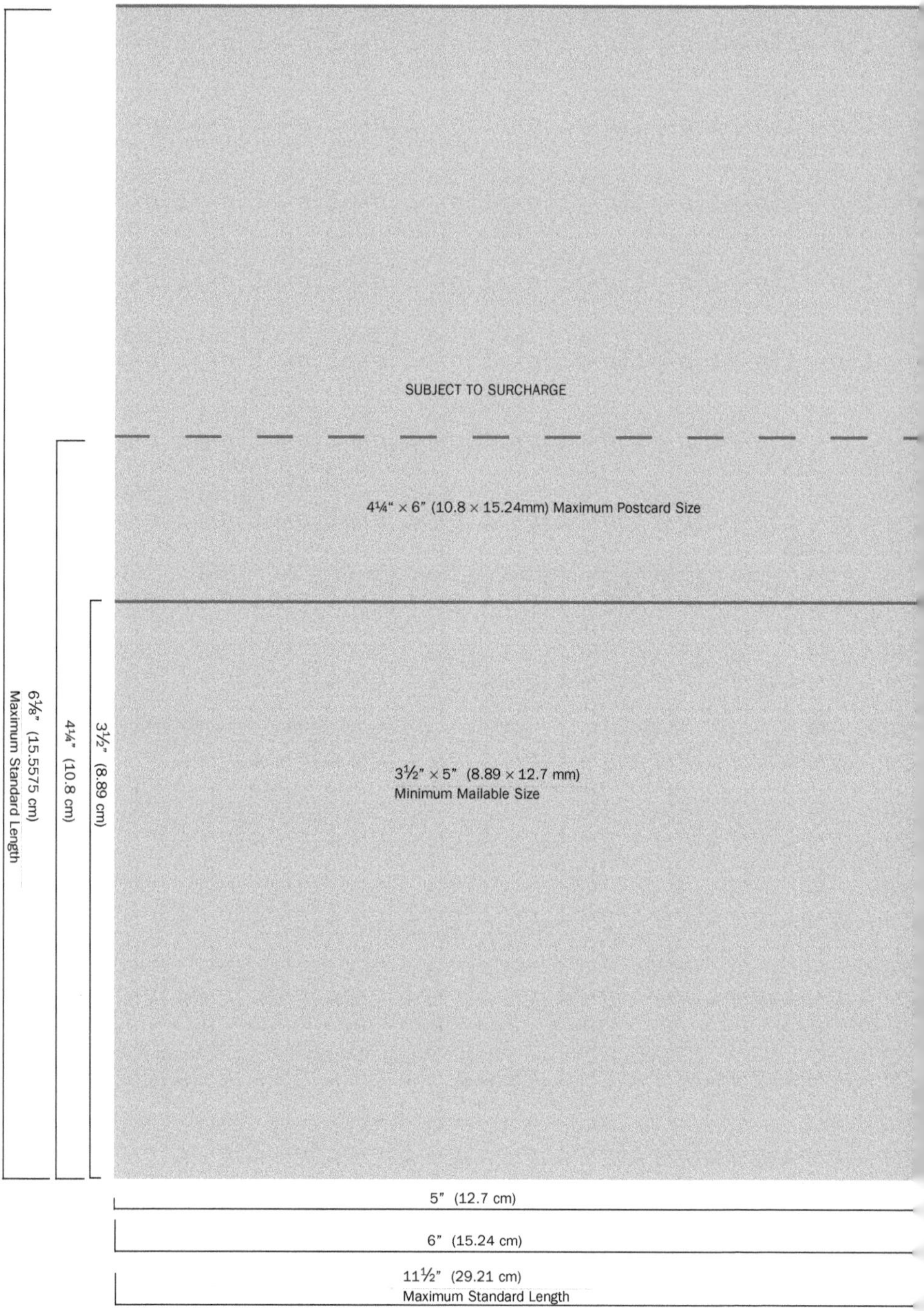

SUBJECT TO SURCHARGE

4¼" × 6" (10.8 × 15.24mm) Maximum Postcard Size

3½" × 5" (8.89 × 12.7 mm)
Minimum Mailable Size

6⅛" (15.5575 cm)
Maximum Standard Length

4¼" (10.8 cm)

3½" (8.89 cm)

5" (12.7 cm)

6" (15.24 cm)

11½" (29.21 cm)
Maximum Standard Length

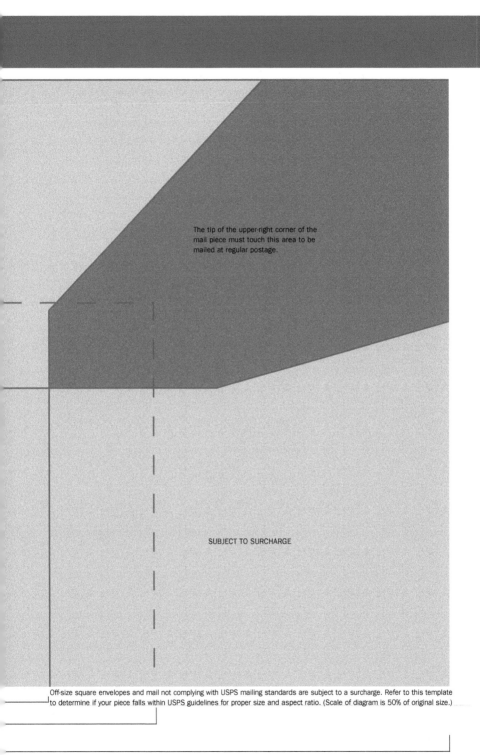

The tip of the upper-right corner of the mail piece must touch this area to be mailed at regular postage.

SUBJECT TO SURCHARGE

Off-size square envelopes and mail not complying with USPS mailing standards are subject to a surcharge. Refer to this template to determine if your piece falls within USPS guidelines for proper size and aspect ratio. (Scale of diagram is 50% of original size.)

THICKNESS REQUIREMENTS FOR FLAT MAIL (UNITED STATES)

The USPS also has requirements for the thickness of cards, envelopes, and flats.

Letter envelopes: Must be ¼ inch (6.35 mm) or less in thickness.

Large envelopes or flats: Must be 0.009 inch (0.2286 mm) and no more than ¾ inch (19.05 mm) in thickness.

Postcards: Cards measuring 4¼" × 6" (10.795 mm × 15.25 mm) or less must be printed on stock that is at least 0.007 inch (0.1778 mm) or a basis weight of at least 75#. Postcards larger than 4¼" × 6" (10.795 mm × 15.25 mm) must have a thickness of 0.009 inch (0.2286 mm) or a basis weight of at least 80#.

SIZE REQUIREMENTS FOR PACKAGES (UNITED STATES)

Merchandise, catalogs, tubes, and other items not meeting the description of a letter, postcard, or a flat are categorized as either bound printed material (books, catalogs, and other publications) or packages. Publications must not exceed 15 lb. (6.804 kg) per unit. Packages must not exceed 70 lb. (31.752 kg) or measure more than 130 inches (330.2 mm) in combined length and distance around the thickest part.

If your package weighs less than 1 lb. (0.46 kg) you can drop it into a collection box. But, anything over 1 lb. (0.46 kg) must be handed to your letter carrier or taken to a post office.

RATE CLASSIFICATIONS AND DELIVERY TIME FOR DOMESTIC MAIL (UNITED STATES)

USPS mailing services are classified by type of mailing and delivery time. Bulk discounts are also available. The following is a list of basic rate classifications and the delivery options available within each. (The services and their requirements listed below are current at the time of publication. Check with a postal agent or the USPS website at www.usps.com for updates.)

LETTERS, POSTCARDS, PERIODICALS

Express: Premium delivery service provides guaranteed one- to two-day delivery for documents that will fit within USPS Express envelopes. Pricing is calculated on weight and distance. Signature proof of delivery and tracking is available.

Priority: Ensures an average two- to three-day delivery for packages up to 70 lb. (31.752 kg) and measuring up to 108 inches (2743 mm) in combined length and distance around the thickest part. Pricing is calculated on weight and distance.

First Class Mail: Used primarily for correspondence, this option is available for letters, envelopes, and postcards weighing 13 ounces (368.5435 gm) or less. Delivery is ensured within one to three days.

Periodical Mail: Newspapers, magazines, and newsletters qualify for this discounted rate with an average of one- to seven-day delivery. No special services are available for this option.

Business Reply Mail: This service lets the sender pay for the recipient's response by establishing an account that covers their mailing costs. Users pay an annual fee, receive a permit, a permit number, and pay an additional amount for each response they receive.

PACKAGE STANDARDS FOR MAILING

Choose a box with enough room for cushioning materials. If you are reusing a box, cover all previous labels and markings with heavy black marker or adhesive labels. Tape the opening of your box and reinforce all seams with 2-inch (5.08 mm) -wide tape. Use clear or brown packaging tape, reinforced packing tape or paper tape. Do not use cord, string, or twine. They can get caught in mail-processing equipment.

LETTERS, POSTCARDS, PERIODICALS (cont.)

Bulk Rate: Discounted rates are available for large mailings with an average two- to nine-day delivery within the continental U.S. Presorting and other preparatory work is required, as well as a permit number and an annual mailing fee. Minimums and size requirements vary depending on the pieces being mailed.

- Standard Mail: A minimum of 200 pieces or 50 lb. (22.68 kg) per mailing is required. Pieces must weigh less than 16 ounces (453.592 gm).

- First Class Mail: A minimum of 500 pieces per mailing is required. Pieces must meet size and weight requirements for first class mail: Up to 13 ounces (368.543 gm).

- Parcel Post: A minimum of 50 pieces per mailing is required. Pieces must meet size and weight requirements for Parcel Post: Up to 130 inches (3302 mm) combined length and distance around the thickest part; up to 70 lb. (31.752 kg).

- Presorted Library Mail: A minimum of 300 pieces is required. Pieces must meet size and weight requirements for Library Mail: Up to 108 inches (2743 mm) combined length and distance around the thickest part; up to 70 lb. (31.752 kg).

- Presorted Media Mail: A minimum of 300 pieces is required. Pieces must meet size and weight requirements for Media Mail: Up to 108 inches (2743 mm) combined length and distance around the thickest part; up to 70 lb. (31.752 kg).

- Carrier Route Bound Printed Matter: A minimum of 300 pieces is required. Pieces must meet weight requirements for Carrier Route Bound Printed Matter: Up to 40 lb. (18.144 kg).

PACKAGES

Bound Printed Matter: Catalogs, directories, and other permanently bound sheets of promotional or editorial material qualify for this rate category. Delivery ranges two to nine days. Weight limit is up to 15 lb. (6.804 kg) per piece.

Library Rate: Special, discounted rate for educational groups, nonprofit organizations, and other qualifying institutions.

Media Mail (also called Book Rate): Cost-efficient way to mail books, sound recordings, videotapes, printed music as well as CDs, DVDs, and disks. Media mail cannot contain advertising. Weight limit is up to 70 lb. (31.752 kg). Delivery ranges from two to nine days.

Parcel Post: Includes boxes, tubes, and rolls. Most economic option for mailing small and large packages weighing up to 70 lb. (31.752 kg) and measuring up to 130 inches (330.2 mm) in combined length and distance around the thickest part.

Parcel Select: Discounted rate for large volumes of package shipments.

Rate Classifications and Delivery Time for International Mail

These rates and delivery times apply to international mail. (The services and their requirements listed below are current at the time of publication. Check with a postal agent or the USPS website at www.usps.com for updates.)

Global Express Guaranteed: Guaranteed delivery within two to three days to more than 200 countries. Pricing is calculated on weight and distance. Signature, proof of delivery, and tracking are available.

Global Express Mail: Delivery within three to five days to more than 190 countries. Return receipt and tracking are available.

Global Priority Mail: Economical option offers delivery within four to six days to 51 countries. Limited to envelopes and packages weighing up to 4 lb. (1.8144 kg).

EXTRA USPS SERVICES

The USPS also offers a range of services that can be added on at an additional cost to the basic cost of mailing a letter or package:

COD (Collect on Delivery): Allows the postal service to collect the postage and price of an item from the recipient and give it to the mailer. The addressee must order the goods.

Certified Mail: Provides proof of mailing at time of mailing and the date and time of delivery or attempted delivery. Return receipt can be added to confirm delivery.

Delivery Confirmation: Provides the date and time of delivery or attempted delivery.

Signature Confirmation: Provides the date and time of delivery or attempted delivery.

Registered Mail: Provides maximum security. Includes proof of mailing at time of mailing and the date and time of delivery or attempted delivery. Insurance up to $25,000 (£12,500) can be added. Return receipt can be added to confirm delivery.

Insured Mail: Provides coverage against loss or damage up to $5,000 (£2,500).

Return Receipt: Provides a postcard with the date of delivery and recipient signature. Must be combined with another extra service. Return receipt for merchandise service is also available.

Certificate of Mailing: Provides evidence of mailing.

Return Receipt for Merchandise: Provides a postcard with the date of delivery and recipient signature. Must be combined with another extra service.

Label Standards for Automated Mailing (United States)

Bulk mailing of envelopes, postcards, and flats can be discounted if they are prepared according to USPS automation standards. Pieces qualifying for automation rates need to meet specific addressing, bar coding, and design standards.

Bar codes: To receive automation rates for cards letters, as well as bulk discounts for parcel post, bound printed matter, and media mail, all the pieces in a mailing must have a delivery point bar code. Automation rate flats must have a delivery point bar code or a ZIP + four bar code. Each piece in a bar coded parcel mailing must have a five-digit bar code. All bar codes must meet placement, size, and legibility standards. Software is available for printing bar coded address labels from a mailing list.

```
#XXXXXXX****3-DIGIT 777
JANE PUBLIC
OCEAN PARK DRIVE
ANYTOWN TX 77777-0000
||.|..||..||.||..|||.|.|..|||.||||.||..|.|.|
```

Bar coded address label for a postcard, letter, or flat.

Address printing: Dark, nonmetallic ink colors must be printed against a white or pastel background to provide adequate print contrast between the printed address and its background. If necessary, areas of dark solid color on a mail piece must be left color free in the address area. To prevent smearing of printed addresses, the USPS recommends using quick-drying inks on a paper stock with a low-gloss surface. If gloss varnish is applied, a varnish-free zone should be reserved for the address area. Addresses should be not be slanted (or skewed) more than 5 degrees relative to the bottom edge of the mail piece.

```
JANE PUBLIC
OCEAN PARK DRIVE
ANYTOWN TX 77777-0000
                        ZIP 77777
```

Bar coded address label for a package.

```
MR & MRS JOHN A SAMPLE
5505 W SUNSET BLVD APT 230
HOLLYWOOD, CA 90028-8521
```

```
||.|..||..||.||.||.||..|||.||||.||..|.|.|
MRS MILDRED DOE
BRAKE CONTROL DIVISION
BIG BUSINESS INCORPORATED
12 E BUSINESS LN STE 209
KRYTON TN 38188-0002
```

Basic address label requirements and quality standards for automated mailings.

Business Reply and Courtesy Reply Mail (United States)

Business Reply (when the permit holder pays postage) and Courtesy Reply Mail (when the sender pays postage) requires a permit number and special envelope or postcard requirements. Art is supplied by the USPS for the indicia (where the permit number appears with Postage Paid), FIM (facing identification mark) and horizontal bars, if applicable. Because placement standards for these elements are very stringent, the USPS recommends that you submit samples of your mail piece to a mail piece design analyst early in the design process to allow time for changes before printing.

MAIL PIECE DESIGN EXPERTISE

Every major U.S. city has a USPS Mail Piece Design Analyst (MPA) on staff to advise on properly designing postcards, envelopes, and packages. MPAs can help you prevent problems before they occur by providing specific recommendations on samples of a mail piece during the design process. They can also offer suggestions at the onset of a project for the most cost-efficient design and mailing option. MPAs also hold regular seminars that are open to the business community at no charge. To locate your regional MPA, contact the main USPS post office branch in your area.

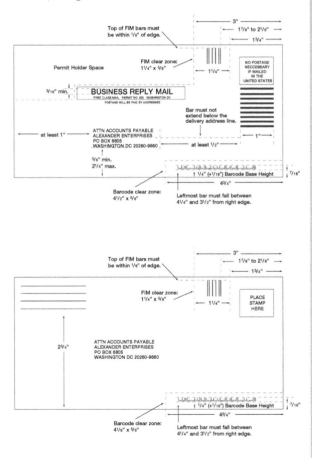

Elements that appear on the face of a Business Reply Mail or Courtesy Reply postcard or envelope must be positioned as shown above.

Sealing Self-Mailers (United States)

Folded self-mailers need to be sealed in way that allows them to be easily fed through the USPS's automated equipment. Consult the diagrams that follow to determine where wafer seals and tabs should be placed.

Double Postcard Size

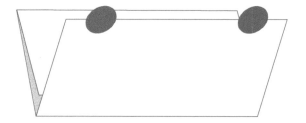

Folded Self-Mailer

Multiple-Sheet Mailer

Short-Fold Mailer

Invitation-Fold Mailer

Booklet with Cover

Spine

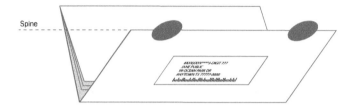

Folded Booklet 1

Spine

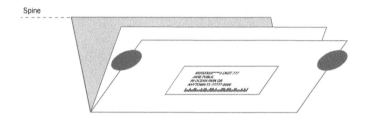

Folded Booklet 2

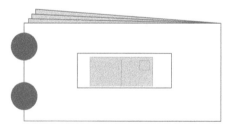

Short-Fold Booklet

POSTAL WEBSITES

Because postal regulations and rates are constantly changing, these websites can help keep you up to date on mailing procedures, current rates and regulations, as well as a rate calculator and other features. Some sites allow users to track mailings, download publications, and print labels.

GENERAL

Universal Postal Union

www.upu.int/

The Universal Postal Union is a department within the United Nations that coordinates worldwide postal services.

Post Info

www.postinfo.net

This website is dedicated to international mailing information providing links to international postal authorities.

INTERNATIONAL POSTAL SERVICE WEBSITES

Åland
Åland Post
www.posten.aland.fi/

Argentina
Correo Argentino
www.correoargentino.com.ar/

Ascension Island
Ascension Island Post Office and Philatelic Bureau
www.postoffice.gov.ac/

Australia
Australia Post
www.auspost.com.au/

Austria
Austrian Postal Services: PTA—Post and Telekom Austria
www.pta.at/

Belgium
De Post—La Poste—Die Post
www.post.be/

Bermuda
Bermuda General Post Office
www.bermudapostoffice.com/

Brazil
Correios (Postal Administration of Brazil)
www.correios.com.br/

Brunei Darussalam
Brunei Postal Services Department
www.post.gov.bn/

Bulgaria
Bulgarian Posts
www.bgpost.bg/

Cambodia
Ministry of Posts
www.mptc.gov.kh/

Canada
Canada Post/Postes Canada
www.canadapost.ca

Channel Islands
Guernsey Post Limited
www.guernseypost.com/

Chile
Correos de Chile
www.correos.cl/

China
China Post
chinapost.gov.cn/english/

Costa Rica
Correos de Costa Rica
www.correos.go.cr/

Croatia
Hvratska Posta
www.posta.hr/

Cyprus
Cyprus Postal Services
www.pio.gov.cy/dps/index.html

Czech Republic
Ceska Posta
www.cpost.cz/

Denmark
Post Danmark
www.postdanmark.dk/

Estonia
Eesti Post
www.post.ee/

Faroe Islands
Postverk Føroya
www.stamps.fo

Fiji
Post Fiji
www.postfiji.com.fj/

Finland
Suomen Posti Oy
www.posti.fi/

France
La Poste française
www.laposte.fr

French Polynesia
Philatelic Center
www.tahiti-postoffice.com

Germany
Deutsche Post
www.deutschepost.de/postagen/

Greece
Hellenic Post
www.elta-net.gr

Honduras
Correos de Honduras
www.honduras.net/honducor/index.html

Hong Kong
Hongkong Post
www.hongkongpost.com/

Hungary
Posta
www.posta.hu/

Iceland
Íslandspóstur
www.postur.is/

Ireland
An Post
www.anpost.ie/

Isle of Man
Isle of Man Post
www.iompostoffice.com/

Jamaica
Postal Corporation of Jamaica Ltd
www.jamaicapost.gov.jm/

Japan
Postal Services Agency
www.yusei.go.jp/eng/english/english
   index.html

Jordan
Jordan Ministry of Post and
Communications
www.mopc.gov.jo/

Kazakhstan
Kazpost
www.kazpost.kz/kazpost_e.html

Kenya
Postal Corporation of Kenya
www.posta.co.ke/

Latvia
Latvijas pasts/Latvia Post
www.post.lv/

Lesotho
Lesotho Postal Services
www.lps.org.ls/

Lithuania
Lithuania Post
www.post.lt/

Luxembourg
P and T Luxembourg—Postes
www.postes.lu/

Maldives
Maldives Post Ltd
www.maldivespost.com/

Mauritius
Ministry of Information Technology &
Telecommunications—Postal Services
Division
ncb.intnet.mu/mitt/postal/index.htm

Netherlands Antilles
Post Netherlands Antilles
www.postna.com/

New Zealand
New Zealand Post
www.nzpost.co.nz/

Nicaragua
Correos de Nicaragua
www.correos.com.ni/

Norway
Posten
www.posten.no/

Pakistan
Pakistan Post
www.pakpost.gov.pk/

Philippines
Philippine Postal Corporation
www.philpost.gov.ph/

Pitcairn Island
Pitcairn Island Mail & Stamps
www.lareau.org//pitmail.html

Poland
Poczta Polska
www.poczta-polska.pl/

Portugal
Correios de Portugal
www.ctt.pt/

Saint Helena
The Island of St. Helena Post Office and
Philatelic Bureau
www.postoffice.gov.sh/

Singapore
Singapore Post
www.singpost.com.sg/

Slovakia
Slovenska Posta
www.slposta.sk/

South Africa
South African Post Office
www.sapo.co.za/

Sweden
Sweden Post
www.posten.se/

Switzerland
La Poste—La Posta—Die Post
www.post.ch

Tanzania
Tanzania Posts Corporation
www.tanpost.com/

Thailand
Communications Authority of Thailand
www.cat.or.th/

Ukraine
Ukrainian Post Home Page
www.ukrposhta.com/

United Kingdom
Royal Mail
www.royalmail.co.uk

British Forces Post Office
www.bfpo.org.uk/

Royal Mail
www.royalmail.com/
Includes a finder for postcodes and post
offices.

Post Office Reform
www.dti.gov.uk/postalservices/network.htm
News and information on the changes
being brought about in the postal market.

United States
The United States Postal Service
www.USPS.com

○ Chapter 12: Bar Code Standards

GENERAL STANDARDS FOR UPC BAR CODES

Bar codes are a series of horizontal or vertical parallel lines representing a code that can be optically read and interpreted by a bar code scanner. Bar coding is used on packaging to speed up pricing at checkout.

· Bar codes must be positioned in a spot that is highly visible and easily scanned.

· A bar code must be printed at a scale between 85% and 120% of its original size.

· Bar codes must be printed in dark colors (dark shades or blue-black and brown or black) against a solid light colored background. (See the following section, Guide to Color-Correct Bar Coding, for more specific information on which colors are readable when printed on common paperboard surfaces.)

· Bars must be printed in a solid color, not screen values of spot colors or screened blends of process colors.

· Bar codes against a colored field must have a color-free area that extends no less than 3/32" (2.4 m) beyond the printed bar code.

· To guard against ink spread, bars should run vertically across the rollers on a web press.

1⅛"
(1.125")
(29 mm)

1 9/32"
(1.59375")
(41 mm)

100% NOMINAL
Minimum Free Space

GUIDE TO COLOR-CORRECT BAR CODING

The key to printing a bar code that can be optically scanned is selecting a color that contrasts sufficiently with its background that the scanner can distinguish between the bars and the background. Coming up with the right combination means checking the background reflectance value of your substrate and combining it with an ink color that contrasts sufficiently.

These are the reflectance values of some common papers. The lighter the color, the higher its reflectance value:

Substrate	Reflectance Value (%)
Natural Kraft	26–43
Mottled	56–77
Bleached	77–87

Inks have a reflectance value as well. Darker colors have a lower reflectance value than lighter colors. To see if the reflectance value of your ink color is low enough to contrast with the substrate on which it will be printed, check its reflectance value and compare it with the reflectance value of your substrate. The tables following list substrate reflectance values in column A and ink reflectance values in column B for UPC and EAN bar codes. Find the reflectance value of your substrate in column A and read across to column B to find the maximum reflectance value of your ink color. Example: If your substrate is natural kraft with a reflectance value of 31%, the reflectance value of your ink must be 2.5% or less. (A series of charts listing reflectance values of common CMYKcolors follows this section.)

Table 1: UPC Versions A&E and EAN 8 & 13*

Column A	Column B
Background Reflectance (%)	Ink Reflectance (%)
31.6	2.5
35	3.3
40	4.6
45	6.3
50	8.3
55	10.6
60	13.3
65	16.4
70	19.8
75	23.7
80	28.1
85	32.9
90	38.1

*Bar codes for U.S. products are designated as UPC versions A and E. Bar codes for European products are designated as EAN 8 and 13. UPC version E and EAN version 13 are small-scale bar codes intended for use on small products or containers such as lip balm.

(Table 1 was excerpted from The Bar Code Color Book, a book published by Symbology, Incorporated. Contact Symbology for a more complete guide on color-correct bar code printing, including color reflectance values for Pantone® colors, at 800.328.2612 (in Minnesota 612.315.8080).

REFLECTANCE VALUES OF FOUR-COLOR COMBINATIONS ON UNCOATED STOCK

Because colors with a reflectance value of more than 40 have the potential to create scanning problems on a bright white substrate, the following list includes colors with a reflectance value of 40 or less. However, if it's important to use a color not on this list, check with your printer to see if there is a possibility of using it for your bar code printing needs. (Note: All reflectance values must be considered accurate plus or minus 5 percent. Ink quality and printing method will affect reflectance values.)

Color	Reflectance Value (%)	Color	Reflectance Value (%)	Color	Reflectance Value (%)
100C, 70M (Reflex Blue)	3	80Y, 60C	15	50Y, 70C	8
100C (Process Blue)	4	80Y, 70C	13	50Y, 80C	8
100C, 60Y (Green)	5	80Y, 80C	13	50Y, 90C	7
100Y, 30K	40	80Y, 90C	12	50Y, 100C	5
100Y, 40K	28	80Y, 100C	12	40Y, 30C	33
100Y, 50K	19	70Y, 20C	38	40Y, 40C	30
100Y, 60K	16	70Y, 30C	32	P40Y, 50C	21
100Y, 20C	35	70Y, 40C	18	40Y, 60C	17
100Y, 30C	32	70Y, 50C	14	40Y, 70C	8
100Y, 40C	15	70Y, 60C	14	40Y, 80C	8
100Y, 50C	15	70Y, 70C	13	40Y, 90C	7
100Y, 60C	14	70Y, 80C	13	40Y, 100C	5
100Y, 70C	14	70Y, 90C	12	30Y, 30C	32
100Y, 80C	13	70Y, 100C	11	30Y, 40C	27
100Y, 90C	13	60Y, 20C	38	30Y, 50C	20
100Y, 100C	13	60Y, 30C	32	30Y, 60C	15
90Y, 20C	35	60Y, 40C	17	30Y, 70C	12
90Y, 30C	32	60Y, 50C	13	30Y, 80C	7
90Y, 40C	28	60Y, 60C	11	30Y, 90C	5
90Y, 50C	28	60Y, 70C	11	30Y, 100C	3
90Y, 60C	16	60Y, 80C	10	20Y, 30C	37
90Y, 70C	15	60Y, 90C	10	20Y, 40C	30
90Y, 80C	14	60Y, 100C	9	20Y, 50C	27
90Y, 90C	13	50Y, 20C	38	20Y, 60C	16
90Y, 100C	13	50Y, 30C	30	20Y, 70C	10
80Y, 30C	40	50Y, 40C	21	10Y, 30C	37
80Y, 40C	27	50Y, 50C	14	10Y, 40C	33
80Y, 50C	21	50Y, 60C	9	10Y, 50C	24

Color	Reflectance Value (%)	Color	Reflectance Value (%)	Color	Reflectance Value (%)
10Y, 60C	18	100M, 40K	24	90M, 30C	26
10Y, 70C	15	100M, 50K	18	90M, 40C	22
100Y, 5M, 30K	31	100M, 60K	14	90M, 50C	16
100Y, 5M, 40K	22	100M, 70K	11	90M, 60C	14
100Y, 20M, 20C	28	100M, 80K	9	90M, 70C	11
100Y, 30M, 30C	30	90M, 20K	38	90M, 80C	8
100Y, 30M, 50C	16	90M, 30K	31	90M, 90C	6
100Y, 40M, 40C	22	90M, 40K	22	90M, 100C	4
100Y, 40M, 20C	31	90M, 50K	18	80M, 30C	30
100Y, 50M, 20C	29	90M, 60K	12	80M, 40C	25
100Y, 50M. 30C	30	90M, 70K	11	80M, 50C	15
100Y, 60M, 20C	34	90M, 80K	10	80M, 60C	13
100Y, 60M, 30C	23	80M, 30K	32	80M, 70C	10
100Y, 60M, 40C	15	80M, 40K	22	80M, 80C	7
100Y, 70M, 30C	24	80M, 50K	18	80M, 90C	5
100Y, 70M, 40C	14	80M, 60K	12	80M, 100C	4
100Y, 80M. 20C	34	80M, 70K	8	70M, 30C	33
100Y, 80M, 40C	19	70M, 30K	33	70M, 40C	28
80Y, 90M, 40C	18	70M, 40K	23	70M, 50C	20
80Y, 100M, 20C	30	70M, 50K	18	70M, 60C	13
60Y, 100M, 30C	24	70M, 60K	11	70M, 70C	10
60Y, 100M, 50C	14	60M, 30K	35	70M, 80C	7
50Y, 90M, 20C	35	60M, 40K	30	70M, 90C	4
50Y, 90M, 40C	22	60M, 50K	11	70M, 100C	4
40Y, 100M, 40C	26	100M, 10C	38	60M, 30C	33
40Y, 100M, 50C	16	100M, 20C	32	60M, 40C	28
30Y, 100M, 30C	30	100M, 30C	28	60M, 50C	22
30Y, 100M, 50C	17	100M, 40C	18	60M, 60C	13
20Y, 100M, 10C	40	100M, 50C	17	60M, 70C	10
20Y, 100M, 30C	30	100M, 60C	14	60M, 80	7
10Y, 100M, 20C	38	100M, 70C	12	60M, 90C	5
10Y, 100M, 40C	23	100M, 80C	9	60M, 100C	5
100M, 10K	40	100M, 90C	5	50M, 30C	34
100M, 20K	32	100M, 100C	4	50M, 40C	28
100M, 30K	30	90M, 20C	30	50M, 50C	24

Color	Reflectance Value (%)	Color	Reflectance Value (%)	Color	Reflectance Value (%)
50M, 60C	15	30C	39	100C, 10Y, 40K	3
50M, 70C	10	40C	31	100C, 20Y	6
50M, 80C	7	50C	25	100C, 20Y, 10K	5
50M, 90C	5	60C	18	100C, 20Y, 20K	3
50M, 100C	4	70C	15	100C, 20Y, 40K	3
40M, 30C	34	80C	12	60C, 60Y, 10K	8
40M, 40C	27	90C	8	90C, 50Y, 10K	6
40M, 50C	23	30C, 20K	32	90C, 50Y, 20K	6
40M, 60C	16	30C, 40K	16	30C, 60Y	32
40M, 70C	12	30C, 60K	6	100C, 30Y, 10K	3
40M, 80C	11	40C, 20K	30	100C, 30Y, 20K	3
40M, 90C	8	40C, 40K	15	100C, 30Y, 40K	3
40M, 100C	5	40C, 60K	6	100C, 40Y, 10K	4
30M, 30C	36	50C, 20K	28	100C, 40Y, 20K	4
30M, 40C	30	50C, 40K	13	100C, 50Y, 10K	4
30M, 50C	26	50C, 60K	5	100C, 50Y, 20K	2
30M, 60C	19	60C, 20K	27	100C, 50Y, 10K	4
30M, 70C	13	60C, 40K	12	100C, 50Y, 20K	4
30M, 80C	11	60C, 60K	5	40C, 80Y, 30K	13
30M, 90C	8	70C, 20K	26	30C, 90Y, 10K	18
30M, 100C	6	70C, 40K	11	30C, 90Y, 20K	18
20M, 30C	36	70C, 60K	4	30C, 90Y, 30K	17
20M, 40C	30	80C, 20K	25	20C, 100Y, 10K	28
20M, 50C	26	80C, 40K	10	20C, 100Y, 20K	23
20M, 60C	20	80C, 60K	5	30C, 100Y, 10K	20
20M, 70C	14	100C, 20K	3	30C, 100Y, 20K	18
20M, 80C	10	100C, 40K	3	30C, 100Y, 30K	17
20M, 90C	8	100C, 60K			
20M, 100C	6	70M, 100C, 10K			
10M, 40C	35	70M, 100C, 20K			
10M, 50C	25	50M, 100C, 10K			
10M, 70C	10	50M, 100C, 20K			
10M, 80C	8	50M, 100C, 30K			
10M, 90C	7	100C, 10Y, 10K			
10M, 100C	6	100C, 10Y, 20K			

QR CODE STANDARDS

QR Code (Quick Response Code) is a matrix barcode consisting of black modules arranged in a square pattern. Unlike UPC bar codes which can hold up to 20 numeric digits, QR codes can hold up to 7,089 characters and can be encoded with virtually any kind of data (alphanumeric, numeric, byte/binary). Standard QR codes can be customized with color, images and shapes to enhance brand recognition.

GENERATING AND READING QR CODES

QR Code Generators

QR codes are created through QR generators. There are numerous free options. Premium generators offer tracking and analytics. A search for QR code generator on the Internet will yield many options.

Kaywa: generate QR code with tracking, analytics and support qrcode.kkaywa.com

UQR: offers generating capabilities, including customizing the color and format of your codes uqr.me

QR Code Readers

Once you've created your QR code, users will need a QR code Reader, which can be downloaded for any smartphone for free.

iPhone QR Reader Apps: i-nigma, TapReader, QR Scanner, QR Reader

Android QR Reader Apps: ScanLife, i-nigma, QR Droid, Barcode Scanner, mobiScan QR

QR CONTENT

QR Codes could be embedded with information such as:

- URL, email address, link to a video
- Social media (such as Facebook or Twitter)
- Expertise information about your product. For example, a QR code on a wine can provide complex information about the grapes, vineyard, history of the wine and a wine rating.
- Event details (event name, time, geo location and description)
- VCard
- Installation instructions
- Sources for replacement parts and service

- Directions to your business with geo location
- Coupons and special offers
- Recommendations for complementary products and services
- Customer feedback forms

QR Codes could be placed on:

- Business cards, brochures and other marketing materials
- Product tags and packaging
- Convention and event nametags
- Restaurant menus
- Event ticket stubs
- Point-of-sale receipts

Chapter 13: Printing and Finishing

GENERAL GUIDE TO PRINTING PROCESSES

There are many ways of applying ink to paper. The most appropriate option depends on budget, the printing surface, the quantity of the run, and the turnaround time involved. Consult the following list for an overview of the printing methods most commonly available.

Offset Lithography: This is the most commonly used method of printing where an image on a plate is offset onto a rubber blanket cylinder which, in turn, transfers the image to a sheet of paper. The process is based on making the printing image ink receptive and water repellent, while the nonprinting areas are rendered water receptive and ink repellent. Offset presses may have more than one printing unit, with each delivering a different color. They come in a range of sizes and can accommodate single sheets as well as rolls of paper.

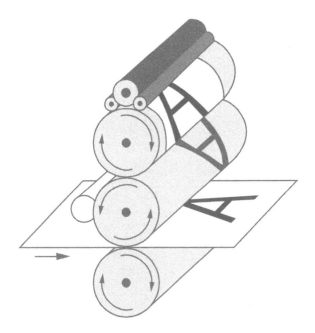

Offset printing involves three rotating cylinders: plate, blanket, and impression. The plate cylinder first contacts the dampening rollers, wetting the plate area. Contact is then made with the inking rollers where the dampened nonimage areas repel the ink. The inked image is then transferred from the plate cylinder to the rubber blanket cylinder. The soft rubber surface of the blanket creates a clear and sharp impression on a range of paper surfaces.

Letterpress: One of the oldest and most basic forms of printing, letterpress uses letters molded from lead that are inked and pressed against the paper. Images and graphics can be applied with an etched plate. Text, imagery, and graphics are locked together on the press bed in a "chase." The process typically yields a soft, inked impression on paper. More time intensive than offset, letterpress printing is most often used for printing art books, invitations and announcements, and other situations where an antique or artistic image is desired.

Gravure: Web presses are fitted with cylinders that carry an etched plate. The plate transfers the inked, etched image directly onto the paper. Gravure offers excellent image reproduction, but because of the expense involved in platemaking, it is usually reserved for extremely large runs such as catalog printing, postage stamps, and packaging applications.

Engraving: Similar to gravure, engraving also involves an etched plate that carries an inked impression. With engraving, the paper is positioned and forced against the plate with tremendous pressure, drawing the ink from the depressed areas on the plate and yielding a slightly embossed surface, with a slightly indented impression on the back of the paper. Limit engraved designs to 4" × 9" (101.6 × 228.6 mm), the size of most engraving plates. Engraving yields sharp imagery and text, but the expense involved in platemaking makes it suitable for long and repeat runs, such as currency and postage stamps. Engraving is often used when a prestigious, formal look is desired for corporate stationery.

Thermography: Similar to engraving in appearance, thermography uses a combination of heat-cured powder and ink to create a raised impression. Thermography costs less than engraving and is often used on business cards and stationery. The process is not appropriate for printing halftones or large areas of color, which are likely to have a pitted or mottled appearance.

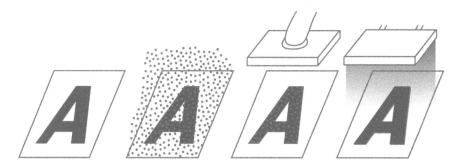

Thermography involves applying powder to a slow-drying ink. After the excess powder is vacuumed away, heat is applied. The curing of the ink and powder causes it to swell, creating a raised impression.

Screen printing: A squeegee is pulled across a silk screen to which a stencil has been applied, forcing the ink onto the surface of the paper or substrate. More labor intensive than offset, screen printing is used for printing on surfaces not accommodated on an offset press, such as fabric, industrial papers, acrylic, and metal. The process can be done by hand or by machine. Halftone screens need to be coarse, ranging from 65 to 85 lpi. (See Chapter 4, Imaging and Color, for more information on halftone screens.) Often used for printing signage, bottles, garments and other unusual shapes and surfaces.

Screen printing involves forcing ink through a mesh screen onto a substrate beneath the screen. The stenciled area on the screen acts as a mask, preventing ink from passing through the nonimage areas of the mesh.

Flexography: Web presses are fitted with rubber or soft plastic plates with a raised impression for printing on unusual surfaces not appropriate for offset printing. Substrates include kraft paper, tissue, vinyl, and other types of plastic. Flexography is often used for printing toilet tissue, bread wrappers, plastic bags, and other types of packaging as well as cartons, shopping, and grocery bags.

Digital: Often referred to as "on-demand" printing because of its quick turnaround time, digital printing is quickly becoming a viable alternative to traditional offset printing. It is particularly useful for printing short-run (under 1,000) four-color jobs where set-up time and charges would make traditional four-color offset cost prohibitive. The digital process differs from offset in that it is a toner-on-paper process, rather than an ink-on-paper process. Because the color sits on top of the paper, it can flake off at folds or spines. Digital printing also places limitations on sheet sizes, with many presses limited to paper sizes of 11" × 17" (279.4 × 431.8 mm) or less, as well as the types of papers that can be used. When using a digital process, check to see what size and basis weight restrictions may be involved.

Holography: Holographic or three-dimensional imagery is created by digitizing an image so that it is divided into several layers. The process involves bouncing laser beams off of mirrors and focusing them onto a photosensitive plate. The holographic design is then embossed onto coated white paper that is metallized for a shimmery effect. Holography requires working closely with specialized vendors over a period of several weeks, and set-up charges can make the process cost prohibitive for small-run projects. Holography is used on credit cards, trading cards, book covers, beverage packaging, and other situations where high-volume makes it a cost-effective option.

Lenticular printing: The process creates an animated effect where images flip back and forth when viewed from different angles. (For instance, a photograph of an individual with an eye that actually winks). It is achieved by laminating a plastic lens over two or more images that have been digitized and broken down into a series of dots. Producing a lenticular image requires working closely with a lenticular vendor to produce digital imagery that meets their requirements. The expense and time involved make lenticular printing suitable for mass-production situations such as product manufacture and packaging but unrealistic for small-run or short-turnaround projects.

TRAPPING TOLERANCES

Keeping colors in register means aligning them on press exactly as they have been specified. But when two colors are adjoining, there is always the possibility that a colorless gap may occur between the colors if registration isn't exact. To compensate for this, a slight overlap, called a *trap,* is created between the two colors. The amount of trapping will vary, depending on the absorbency of the paper or substrate and printing method used. Although most commercial printers take responsibility for creating traps, it's useful to know how trapping tolerances can vary for different printing methods. The following chart shows typical trapping tolerances for a variety of printing processes and substrates:

Printing Method	Substrate	Trap (inches)	Trap (mm)	Trap (pt.)
Sheetfed offset	uncoated paper	0.003	0.08	0.25
Sheetfed offset	coated paper	0.003	0.08	0.25
Web offset	coated paper	0.004	0.10	0.30
Web offset	uncoated paper	0.005	0.14	0.40
Web offset	newsprint paper	0.006	0.15	0.45
Gravure	coated paper	0.003	0.08	0.25
Flexography	coated paper	0.006	0.15	0.45
Flexography	newsprint paper	0.008	0.20	0.60
Flexography	kraft/corrugated paper	0.010	0.25	0.75
Screen printing	fabric	0	0	0
Screen printing	paper	0.006	0.15	0.45

TYPES OF OFFSET LITHOGRAPHY

Offset lithography is the most widely used method of printing. The process can be broken down into two basic categories: sheetfed offset and web offset. Print shops are often set up to specialize in one of these two types of offset printing. Consult the following descriptions for further information on which method is most appropriate for a specific project.

Sheetfed Offset: Individual sheets of paper pass through the press. Small, sheetfed presses print on papers smaller than 18 inches (457.2 mm) in width and are used for printing fliers, letterheads, envelopes, and business cards. Larger presses that accommodate paper sizes ranging from 19" × 25" (482.6 × 635 mm) to 55" × 78" (1397 × 1981.2 mm) allow printers to run larger jobs, such as posters or book signatures, or gang several pieces on one sheet. Sheetfed presses generally work best for small- to mid-size press runs or when quality is critical.

Web Offset: Paper going through a web press is fed from a roll and is cut into sheets after printing. Small-sized web presses that accommodate paper widths of up to 9 inches (228.6 mm) are used for printing business forms and other small pieces. Larger presses (called full web presses) that run rolls from 35 inches to 40 inches (889 to 1016 mm) wide are used for publications. Full web presses can print sixteen-page signatures on a trim size that is typically 23" × 35" (635 mm × 889 mm). Web presses are designed to print hundreds of impressions per minute and many thousands per hour and are suitable for high-volume publications such as newspapers, magazines, and catalogs. Many presses also come equipped with heating units to speed up ink drying time as well as folding and binding units to expedite production.

Printers will often gang several pieces on a single sheet, such as fitting nine 4½" × 6¼" (114 × 159 mm) invitations on a 23" × 35" (584 × 889 mm) sheet of paper.

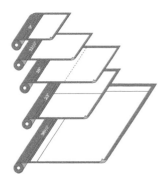

Web presses are categorized according to the size of the paper rolls they run. Small presses called *form webs* are used for business forms, while large presses called *full webs* are used for publications. In-between sizes include miniweb, half web, and three-quarter web presses.

CUTTING AND TRIMMING

Because most pressruns use paper slightly larger than the finished piece or gang several pieces on a single sheet, waste must be cut away and pieces cut apart. All straight line cuts are called *trims*. Trim lines are indicated by crop marks so that whoever is trimming the job will know where pieces needed to be cut. Trimming a job is included in the cost of printing, and is not the same as perforating, making die-cuts, drilling, or punching holes. These applications are performed at an additional charge. For more information on perforating, die-cuts, drilling and punching, see Finishing Techniques.

FINISHING TECHNIQUES

Finishing techniques are applied after a job is printed to create a special effect that can't be achieved with ink. They also include special cuts and trims that are part of the design or applications that make a piece easy to fold, tear, or ready for binding.

Embossing: Paper is pressed between two molds called *dies*, typically made from magnesium or brass. The molding of the paper between the dies results in a raised impression. If an impression is molded so that it is lower than the paper's surface, it is called a *deboss*. Embossing can be combined with a printed image or foil stamping to enhance the three-dimensional appearance of the image. An embossed impression made independent of a printed or foil-stamped image is called a *blind emboss*. Soft, uncoated papers generally take a better embossed impression than hard or smooth coated papers. Papers with a textured finish are often preferred because they render a smooth impression that contrasts favorably with the surrounding texture. Text and light to midweight cover stocks work best. Lightweight bonds and writing papers tend to be too thin to show off an emboss, whereas, heavier cover weight stocks can be too thick to be molded. Embossing is frequently used on brochure covers, stationery, business cards, and pocket folders.

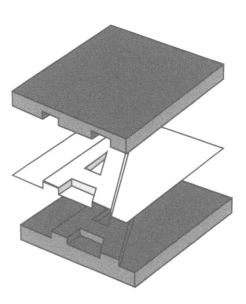

Embossing requires two matched dies (male and female counterparts). One of the dies is heated as the paper is pressed between, resulting in a raised impression.

Foil stamping: Paper is stamped with a hot die that presses a thin plastic film carrying colored pigment against the paper. Plastic film comes in more than 200 colors, including pearlized effects and metallics, as well as clear foil stamps that mimic the look of a varnish. Because the process can render a completely opaque image, foil stamping is often used to apply a light-colored image against a dark-colored paper. In addition to applications on any paper that can withstand heat, foil stamping is also suitable for pens and pencils, cloth book covers, vinyl binders, toys, and other nonpaper applications. When foil stamping is combined with embossing, it's called *foil embossing*. The process involves applying foil first and then the emboss.

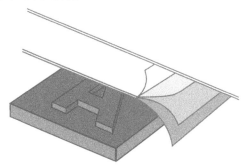

Foil stamping involves applying foil to paper with a heated die. The pigment bonds with the paper, rendering a smooth image.

Die-cutting: The process includes making cuts in a printed sheet in a configuration that will allow it to be used or assembled into a functional piece, such as a door hanger, pocket folder, or carton. Die-cutting also includes cuts that enhance a piece's design appeal, such as die-cutting a holiday greeting card in the shape of a Christmas tree. Dies are typically made from bending metal strips with a sharpened edge into the desired shape and mounting them onto a wooden block. The metal strips, called *rules*, are higher than the wooden backing, creating a cutting edge that works much like a cookie cutter. Printers often keep a supply of standard dies for common items such as pocket folders and table tents. Cutting labels and decals from printed paper, but not its backing, is called *kiss die cutting*. Sheets printed this way allow the label or decal to be peeled away from the backing.

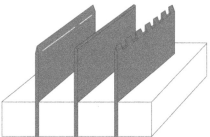

Shown, from left to right, are dies for cutting, scoring, and perforating.

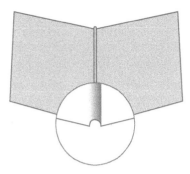

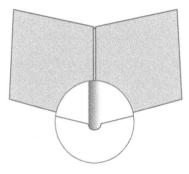

When a piece is scored, the fold should always be made with the ridge or hinge on the inside for minimum stretch.

Scoring: To facilitate folding, a crease is applied using the metal edge of either a rule or a wheel so that an embossed ridge on the paper is formed. Heavy text and cover stocks should always be scored. Scoring is especially important to prevent cracked ink on fold lines when using coated stocks with heavy ink coverage.

Perforating: Perforating involves punching a line of holes to make tearing easier. It can be done as part of the binding process to make signatures easier to fold before they are bound and trimmed as part of a publication or as a means of facilitating tear-offs on pieces that include response vehicles, such as business reply cards.

Drilling/punching: Pieces that are ring or post bound require holes ranging between ⅛" and ¼". Commercial printers and binderies use a drill to make these holes according to size and placement specifications. Spiral and plastic comb binding require punching holes, a process that costs a bit more than drilling.

OFFSET INKS

Most purchasers of printed products don't give ink a second thought beyond specifying a color. Although it's a good practice to let your printer choose an ink that's appropriate for the paper (or other substrate) and function of the piece, it's worthwhile to know how some inks perform as compared to others.

High gloss: Ink formulation includes a high content of varnish for maximum sheen. Most effective when used on coated and cast-coated stocks. Not appropriate for heat drying, which can reduce gloss.

Heat set: Quick-drying inks used in web offset. Ink solvents are vaporized as they pass through a heating chamber at the end of the press. The ink is then set as it passes through cooling rolls.

Metallic: Made from a mixture of metal dust and varnish, metallic inks have the greatest effect on coated paper. They have a tendency to rub off if the ink has been laid down thickly. Some metallics, such as copper, can also have a tendency to tarnish. An overlay of varnish can minimize these problems.

Fluorescent: More opaque and vibrant than standard inks, fluorescents can also be mixed with process inks to increase their vibrancy. Fluorescents don't always retain their colorfastness as long as standard inks and may not be suitable for pieces with a long shelf life or those that will be exposed to sunlight.

Vegetable-based: Inks made either entirely from or from some percentage of vegetable oil rather than petroleum (e.g. cottonseed, linseed, soy, etc). Vegetable-based inks tend to release fewer VOCs (volatile organic compounds, see glossary). Vegetable-based inks are capable of performing just as well as an ink that is petroleum-based, however they may handle differently on press, and some printers may charge a premium for their use.

VARNISHES AND PROTECTIVE LIQUID COATINGS

Varnishes and other liquid coatings are applied to protect the inked surface of a piece or to enhance a design, either by dulling or applying a glossy finish to the surface. A range of protection and aesthetic possibilities exists, with each type of coating offering its own set of advantages. As a general rule, varnishes and liquid coatings work best on coated papers. They tend to be absorbed into uncoated papers, creating a mottled appearance.

Coatings also need to be compatible with the type of ink used. Metallics, and other pigments as well as other ingredients in the ink may present a problem. Be sure to let your printer know what type of coating or laminate will be used to ensure that a compatible ink is used for the project.

Spot varnish: A clear coating is applied on press or in line, just as another ink would be to isolated areas on a piece. Spot varnish costs no more than another ink color would cost. Spot varnish comes in glossy or dull finishes and can also be lightly tinted with other inks. Spot gloss varnish is often used to enhance photographs and other imagery by giving them a high sheen and richness similar to the effect achieved with the high-gloss paper used for photographic prints. In contrast, dull varnish is often applied only to areas of text on a glossy coated paper to prevent glare and make photographs and other imagery stand out. It offers little protection against scuffing, dirt, and spills but some protection against fingerprints. Spot varnish can also prevent flaking and rub-off when applied to metallic inks.

Aqueous coating: A glossy coating made from a mix of polymers and water that is often applied to magazine and brochure covers as a means of protection against scuffing, dirt, and water. Aqueous coatings are applied as a flood varnish, meaning that the entire sheet is covered, at the end of the pressrun. Aqueous coatings require a special coating unit that is usually installed at the end of the press, and they cost about twice as much as a spot varnish.

Ultraviolet or UV coating: An ultraviolet light-cured process that involves a plastic liquid, ultraviolet coatings offers more protection and a higher degree of gloss than aqueous coating. Some printers can apply ultraviolet coating in line, but it is most often applied as a separate operation, often by screen printing as either a flood or spot varnish or applied with a roller unit as a flood varnish. The roller-applied process is more economical for long runs, whereas, screen printing is more cost-effective for short runs. When applying UV coatings, use wax-free inks. Although UV coating is available in a dull finish, it is more expensive than gloss. The durable finish of ultraviolet coating is most often used on pocket folders, book covers and table tents. Because its hard plastic surface may crack at fold lines, care should be taken when scoring and folding UV-coated pieces.

Laminates

Laminating offers the best protection of all methods, yielding an exceptionally strong surface that repels moisture that can even be washed. The process involves adhering a layer of polyester, polypropylene, or nylon film to one or both sides of the printed sheet. Laminates are available in thicknesses from 0.001 inch (0.0251 mm) to 0.010 inch (0.251 mm) in both gloss and dull finishes, as well as a satin finish that falls in between. Thinner films are more appropriate for book covers and packaging, whereas, thicker films are better suited for menus, displays, and name tags. Laminating costs more than varnishes and liquid coatings, with the exception of matte UV.

When selecting the most appropriate laminate for a project, keep the following considerations in mind:

Nylon laminates: These durable laminates are the most expensive, but their porosity helps prevent paper curl by allowing gasses and moisture to leave the underlying paper. Nylon laminates are recommended for lightweight substrates such as paperback covers and applications where metallic inks are involved.

Polyester laminates: Their hard surface and median price makes polyester laminates appropriate for case-bound books and situations where durability and longevity are important.

Polypropylene laminates: Laminates made of this material are often used on dust jackets and packaging. Although they are softer than other laminates and more likely to be scuffed and scratched, polypropylene laminates are the least expensive. Polypropylene laminates can also be applied to lightweight substrates and surfaces printed with metallic inks without fear of curling.

INSERTING EXTRAS AND/OR OVERSIZED PAGES

Throw-outs, gatefolds, tip-ins and tip-ons provide ways of inserting additional materials into publications.

Gatefolds: folded sheet of four panels that is bound into a publication. Panels fold into a spine with parallel folds. Used in publications to provide extra space (especially useful for panoramic vista images).

Throw-outs: half a gatefold where a folded sheet is bound into a publication that opens out to only 1 side. The throw-out sheet must be smaller than the actual publication so it can be nested when folded.

Tip-in: a single page wrapped around the central fold and glued along the binding edge.

Tip-on: a page or other element (such as a reply card or membership card) pasted into a publication. Can be located anywhere on the host page and may be temporary or permanent.

PROOFING METHODS

Proofs help designers and others know, before beginning press production, how a piece will look and feel when it has been printed and assembled. They also serve as a means of checking how a digital file will print and ensuring that type, imagery, and color will print as specified.

A broad range of proofing possibilities exists. Which method you choose depends largely on what aspect of a job is being checked. In many cases, one type of proof will be adequate in the early stages of a job, whereas, others will be more useful as the job progresses.

Paper dummy: A paper dummy is a nonprinted sample assembled to project specifications with the paper that has been specified for the job. Although paper dummies do not show how a job will look when printed, they are useful for showing how bulky a document will be and how much it will weigh, if mailing costs are a consideration. Paper dummies are useful when making paper choices for pocket folders, direct mail pieces, and all other types of publications.

Ink drawdowns: Provided by the ink supplier to the printer, ink drawdowns are used for determining how the ink and paper will interact before going on press. Generally prepared in 12" × 6" (304.8 × 152.4 mm) strips, drawdowns are often used to determine absorption rates on uncoated papers and for matching critical colors, such as a corporate colors, on different types of papers.

Bluelines: Photosensitive paper is combined and exposed with film negatives for a job to give a one-color (blue) representation of how the job will print. Bluelines work well for checking the placement of text and images, cropping and image size as well as crossovers, folds, and page sequencing. They are not suitable for checking color or image quality. They can only be generated when film negatives are produced as part of the job. Also called *Dyluxes*.

Analog color proofs: Analog color proofs involve overlays, made directly from film negatives that record each color on a separate sheet of clear polyester film. The films are taped or laminated together in register to give a representation much like a color print. Dyes for these proofs are matched to inks to simulate the finished, printed piece. Because they are made from the negatives that will print the final job, analog proofs have long been regarded as the most accurate means of determining imaging and color accuracy. Cromalin and Color Key are both brand names for this type of proofing system.

Digital proofs: Digital proofs range from simple black-and-white laser prints generated from a studio printer to sophisticated color proofs that simulate how a job will look when it is finally produced on press. Digital proofs are your only option if offset plates are generated directly from digital files without producing negatives— an option commercial printers are increasingly turning to as digital prepress technology becomes more sophisticated and color accuracy more reliable. Processes include prints generated by laser, thermal, dye sublimation, or ink-jet printers.

○ Chapter 14: Greening Graphic Design

THE SHIFT TOWARD SUSTAINABLE PRACTICE

Sustainable graphic design can provide an opportunity to tap into an emerging market, work with clients who have similar values, and reduce the negative impact that print design has on the environment. For most designers, the transition to sustainable practice begins with a shift in thinking and the adoption of better production methods but will not require a complete alteration of their design process. This chapter will explain the basics of environmentally and socially responsible communication design and provide information and targets for how designers can become sustainable practitioners.

Sustainability refers to the balanced use of natural, social, and economic resources for the continued health of the planet for future generations. This means minimizing the use of processes and materials that will jeopardize the ability of future generations to survive and thrive.

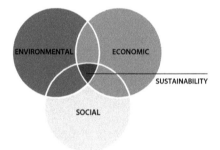

Related Terms:

Green Design, Ecofriendly, and Ecodesign are frequently used in place of, or in addition to, the term sustainable when referring to processes, concepts, and materials that put value on environmental responsibility. It is important to understand that there is a distinction between something that has been labeled green or that uses the prefix eco- and the term sustainable. The former primarily refers to a concern for the environment while sustainability refers to a balance of social, economic, and environmental capital.

Socially Conscious Design

There is little point in making a hard distinction between socially and environmentally con-scious design since sustainability requires the melding of the two. However, there is an emerging specialization in design for social causes and nonprofits. Working with clients that share your values can be a great way of shifting toward sustainable practice.

Sustainable Design Thinking

Subtle shifts in how graphic designers approach projects can significantly shift one's practice in line with sustainable values. Pairing environmentally responsible production with design thinking can be as easy as asking questions about each project you take on and by adhering to the following guidelines.

STEP 1: GREENING YOUR STUDIO
- Use recycled and Forest Stewardship Council (FSC) certified office paper.
- Switch to renewable energy and use compact fluorescent bulbs.
- Educate employees and coworkers about sustainable options.

STEP 2: EVALUATE THE PROJECT
- Does this piece deserve to exist? (Will it serve its intended goal?)
- Can this piece serve dual purposes? Can fewer pieces be printed? Can it be digitally distributed with PDFs?

STEP 3: DESIGN FOR A GREENER SOLUTION
- Adjust size of printed materials to minimize waste on a press sheet.
- Ask for water based adhesives instead of glues with synthetic resins that release VOCs.
- Consider how to the consumer can re-use or recycle the package/product. Include recycling instructions if the materials can be easily recycled.
- Design for minimal ink coverage (effective use of white space).
- Proof on screen when possible.

- Put the recycled logo and other pertinent certifications on the final piece to promote recycling and to educate the consumer.
- Educate clients about sustainable options and advocate for ecofriendly production.

STEP 4: GREEN PRODUCTION
- Use the services of an environmentally responsible printer.
- Use digital or waterless printing when possible.
- Spec recycled or FSC certified paper, ecofriendly bindings, and water-based finishes.

SUSTAINABLE MATERIALS AND PRODUCTION FOR PRINT DESIGN

Specifying environmentally preferable printing processes and materials can greatly reduce the negative impact that graphic designers have on environment and social systems. Paper production and printing are both resource intensive processes. They use a tremendous amount of energy, potentially harmful chemicals, and can negatively affect local air and water quality. Since 75 percent of communications pieces end up in landfills within one year, using the most environmentally responsible paper products and working with a printer that is concerned about energy use and water and air quality is essential.

FORESTRY

As the first step in the lifecycle of paper, commercial forestry and environmental management have an important role to play in designers' abilities to work sustainably. One of the most common misconceptions about forestry is that planting new trees is equivalent to saving forests. That is simply not the case. In the United States, millions of new trees are planted each year, and annual plantings actually exceed the number of trees cut for industrial purposes. However, these plantations do not have the same benefits as natural forests.

Old growth forests, which include boreal and rainforests, are forests that have been allowed to grow naturally for more than one hundred years and that have developed into complete ecosystems containing every stage of tree life as well as the appropriate biodiversity of other plants and animals. Intact forests have not been significantly disturbed by fire, logging, clear cutting, road building, or other human activity. The difference in the environmental and societal benefits of plantation tracts versus old growth forests are enormous, and around the world community groups, nongovernmental organizations (NGOs), and governmental organizations are working to minimize the destruction to the remaining intact forests.

Why Tree Fiber Is Still Needed

It might seem that discontinuing the use of virgin fiber (fiber that comes directly from its organic source) in paper production would be the best way to combat deforestation and illegal logging. Unfortunately, there is not enough recycled waste paper to satisfy global demands nor has any other agricultural crop proved to be a viable alternative to fiber from wood sources. For the foreseeable future there will continue to be a need for forest products from virgin sources.

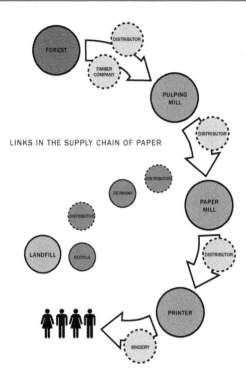

LINKS IN THE SUPPLY CHAIN OF PAPER

In the case of larger companies and integrated mills, many of the following steps may come under the umbrella of one company. However, in some cases there can be up to ten different companies involved in the supply chain of print production.

SUSTAINABLE VOCABULARY

Understanding the relevant terms can be one of the biggest stumbling blocks to adopting sustainable practices. The following are some of the most common terms that designers will encounter when specing paper and reading about sustainability issues.

Agricultural Fibers are harvested from tree-free organic sources that are grown specifically for use in paper production; often bears the Tree Free label.

Agricultural Residues are fibers recovered from annual crops usually planted as food crops or for commercial use (such as corn, sugar cane, and wheat) that is used to make paper. The use of these fibers is usually limited to areas where crops are grown locally.

Carbon Dioxide is a heavy, colorless, odorless gas that results from the combustion of carbon found in organic materials. Carbon dioxide is the gas most closely associated with global climate change.

Chlorine is used in the bleaching process to give paper its white appearance and to remove lignin, a naturally occurring material that can gradually yellow when exposed to sunlight, as in newsprint.

De-inking is the process of removing ink and other contaminants from collected paper. De-inking is usually done at a separate facility and finished fiber is sent to paper manufacturers.

Dioxins are a group of toxic substances that are produced during the paper production processes when pulp is exposed to elemental chlorine. The effects of dioxins on the environment and human health are not fully understood but have been associated with cancer and birth defects.

Effluent is waste in liquid (most often water) that is discharged from a mill, or other manufacturing facility, and can end up in the groundwater.

Elemental Chlorine Free (ECF) indicates fibers that have been bleached without elemental chlorine and is instead made with chlorine derivatives such as chlorine dioxide (CO_2).

The Forest Stewardship Council (FSC) is an independent third-party certifier of sustainably harvested virgin fiber and mixed-use recycled content. To use the FSC logo as an environmental claim on paper, the product must have gone through the FSC chain of custody from an FSC-certified forest, to a paper manufacturer, merchant, and finally printer who has FSC chain-of-custody certification.

Mill Broke is paper waste generated by a mill that can be reused in the manufacturing process. Mill broke may contain a fairly large percentage of recycled content so it is preferable to ask what percentage of the recycled content is derived from postconsumer waste content and where the rest comes from. (Also see *Preconsumer Waste*)

Old Growth, also called intact forests (included in this category are boreal and rainforest), are natural forests that have been allowed to grow naturally over a long period of time (in excess of 100 years) and have developed into complete ecosystems containing every stage of tree life as well as the appropriate biodiversity of other plants and animals.

Postconsumer Waste (PCW) is paper that has been used by the consumer and then collected to make new material (rather than end up in a landfill or incinerator). This is what most people think of as recycled paper.

Preconsumer Waste refers to materials that include trim or scrap from the manufacturing process and printers or even overruns that are reused to make new products. This may account for as much as 20 percent of paper referred to simply as recycled. (Also see *Mill Broke*)

Processed Chlorine Free (PCF) is used to refer to fiber that was not bleached using chlorine or chlorine derivatives during the recycling process but may have been bleached using chlorine during the paper's initial production and, therefore, may not be totally chlorine free.

Recycled Paper is derived from either pre- or postconsumer waste. Recycled pulp can be used to make the same variety and quality of paper stock made from virgin fiber. However, not all recycled material is equal and some fibers (such as cardboard or colored papers) may be better suited for reuse in packaging stock.

TCF and PCF both use benign elements such as oxygen, ozone, or hydrogen peroxide for the bleaching process. Most scientists and environmentalist believe that Totally Chlorine Free production is preferable to Elemental Chlorine Free bleaching.

Totally Chlorine Free (TCF) indicates fibers that have been produced without the use of any chlorine in the bleaching process or is unbleached.

Tree-Free includes paper products made from agricultural residues, nontree fibers, and, more recently, products made from minerals and plastics. *Note: Tree-free does not necessarily denote more environmentally preferable products.*

Volatile Organic Compounds (VOCs) refers to a broad class of organic gasses that includes vapors from solvents, inks, and gasoline. Minimizing or eliminating the use of products that produce VOCs is important because these compounds can react with other materials to form ozone, the major ingredient of smog.

Virgin Fiber refers to paper pulp fiber that is derived directly from its organic source (mostly refers to wood fiber). This material can be an environmentally responsible choice when it is third-party certified (FSC) and comes from sustainably managed forests.

FIBER SOURCING AND PAPER PRODUCTION

The harvesting of trees for pulp production and the conversion of pulp into finished paper are responsible for the bulk of the negative environmental impact made by the paper industry. Paper production and the sourcing of fiber are two of the most important areas to target when adopting sustainable design practices.

Ideally, the paper that you choose should be produced with a combination of post-consumer recycled content and virgin fiber from sustainably managed forests (FSC certified). It should be made without the use of elemental chlorine by a company that uses renewable energy. Targeting these areas may be as simple as comparing different sheet specifications with a knowledgeable printer. However, understanding the touch points for paper production and forestry can make the process easier especially since the minimum criteria for sustainable production are neither stable nor clearly defined.

Sustainable Forestry and the FSC

Each year, thousands of acres of forestland are felled and/or burned for use by the timber industry to make way for agriculture, and to satisfy growing global demand for land by urban populations. CO_2 emissions generated by deforestation make up 20 percent of the annual total. Discontinuing the use of virgin tree fiber (fiber that comes directly from its organic source) in paper production might seem to be the best way to combat deforestation and illegal logging. However, there is currently no crop that has proven to be a viable alternative to fiber from wood sources.

Domtar, a paper company based in Montreal, Canada, uses sustainable logging practices when harvesting trees for pulp and paper production. After timber is harvested, sites are prepared and seeded from the air for regeneration of the Jack pine forest. The seed to regenerate these sites is obtained by cone collectors from the tops of trees felled on cuts. To help maintain natural genetic adaptations in regenerating forest stands, the seed or planting stock produced from the harvested cones is returned to the original ecological seed zone.

Fortunately, the impacts of commercial forestry can be greatly reduced if logging is conducted using sustainable forestry practices. Sustainable forestry is a system of managing both the commercial and environmental benefits of forests while maintaining economic, societal, and environmental values. By choosing paper and timber products from sustainably managed forests, graphic designers can support the environmental and social systems that are found in healthy forests while ensuring that the wood fiber found in the paper products that they use does not come from illegally or improperly harvested land.

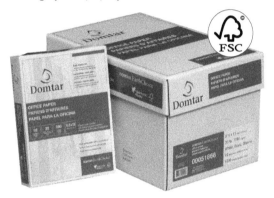

Look for wood products and paper with the FSC logo on it. These boards and Domtar paper were FSC certified by Rainforest Alliance, (an FSC certifying partner organization).

The most respected and widely recognized international certification body for wood products is the Forest Stewardship Council. The FSC uses accredited third-party certifiers to assess the environmental performance of manufacturers, distributors, retailers, and printers against the FSC's performance standards. Using a chain-of-custody system, FSC bases its assessment on ten principles and criteria for forest management that were developed collaboratively by foresters, forestry companies, consumer and retail companies, environmental and social organizations, and community forestry groups.

FSC works with partners around the world to ensure that forest ecosystems remain intact even after an area is logged. It does not certify large-scale logging practices such as clear cutting.

CERTIFICATIONS

One of the easiest ways to achieve more environmentally friendly print production is to use products and services that are assessed using independent third-party certifications. The organizations responsible for the most widely used certifications often use logos and/or visual marks that allow consumers and purchasers to differentiate products quickly. International Organization for Standardizations (ISO), the European Union's Eco-Management and Audit Scheme (EMAS), FSC, and Green E are examples of certifying bodies that guarantee that products or manufacturing processes meet a strict set of criteria. Though well-meaning industry trade groups make information available to consumers, it is easy to overlook or be confused by data or advice that comes from organizations with ties to industry. When choosing products or services, look for certifications that are conducted by independent third-party organizations such as the following.

Chlorine Free Products Association

Chlorine Free Products Association (CFPA) is a certification program for companies that produce chlorine-free products. A product bearing the Totally Chlorine Free (TCF) or Processed Chlorine Free (PCF) emblem is subject to ongoing testing, inspection, and enforcement. Learn more at chlorinefreeproducts.org.

PROCESSED CHLORINE FREE

The Processed Chlorine Free (PCF) seal is reserved for recycled content paper. This includes all recycled fibers used as a feed-stock that meet Environmental Protection Agency guidelines for recycled or postconsumer content. PCF papers have not been rebleached with chlorine-containing compounds. A minimum of 30 percent postconsumer content is required.

TOTALLY CHLORINE FREE

Totally Chlorine Free (TCF) is reserved for virgin fiber papers. TCF papers do not use pulp produced with chlorine or chlorine-containing compounds as bleaching agents.

EMAS

FSC

EMAS
The European Union Eco-Management and Audit Scheme (EMAS) is a management tool for companies and other organizations to evaluate, report, and improve their environmental performance. Learn more at www.ec.europa.eu/environment/emas.

FSC
Forest Stewardship Council (FSC) is a nonprofit international organization established to promote the responsible management of the world's forests. Products carrying the FSC label are independently certified to assure consumers that they come from forests that are managed to meet the social, economic, and ecological needs of present and future generations. Learn more at www.fsc.org (main site) and www.fsc-paper.org (list of FSC-certified papers).

green-e.org

GREEN E
The Green E logo identifies products made by companies that purchase certified renewable energy to offset a portion or all of their electricity use. Renewable energy types include but are not limited to wind power, solar power, low-impact hydropower, and biomass. Learn more at www.green-e.org.

ISO 9000 AND 14000 (NO LOGO TO DATE)
The International Standards Organization (ISO) is a nongovernmental organization made up of a network of the national standards institutes of 157 countries, which all participate in the development of international market-driven standards for industry.

ISO 9000 and 14000 are quality and environmental management standards that a company may choose to adopt. A company's performance is evaluated against the ISO's conformity assessment. ISO 9000 means that the organization in question has committed to enhance customer satisfaction by meeting customer and applicable regulatory requirements. ISO 14000 is a family of certifications that mean that the organization or company is committed to minimizing its harmful effects on the environment caused by its activities and continually improving its environmental performance. Learn more at www.iso.org.

GREEN SEAL
Green Seal is an independent nonprofit organization dedicated to safeguarding the environment and transforming the marketplace by promoting manufacture, purchase, and use of environmentally responsible products and services. Printing and writing paper that are Green Seal certified have met rigorous criteria for product-specific performance, recycled content, production process, and packaging requirements. Learn more at www.greenseal.org.

Energy Conservation and Renewables

Energy sourcing and conservation are important variables for designers who want to work sustainably and can be targeted in the office, at the printer, and with materials chosen for production. Since paper production and printing are energy-intensive processes, it is particularly important that mills and printers utilize energy from renewable resources and conserve where possible.

Common Sources of Renewable Energy

- Solar
- Wind
- Landfill gas
- Biomass
- Geothermal
- Low-impact hydro

Renewable Energy for Paper Production

Btu of Energy Used in Paper Production

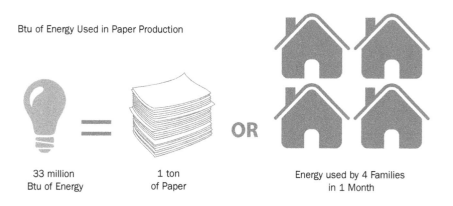

| 33 million Btu of Energy | 1 ton of Paper | Energy used by 4 Families in 1 Month |

On average, paper mills use 33 million Btu of energy to produce 1 ton of paper—approximately the same amount of energy used by four U.S. families in one month.

Paper mills consume about 33 million Btu of energy to produce 1 ton of paper or paperboard. Some mills can make their own power from waste generated during the pulping process. (This may be considered renewable, but it is worth asking about air pollution if waste burning is part of the process.) Mills that don't include pulping facilities and environmentally conscious printers may purchase energy from renewable sources. Renewable energy is a good alternative to power generated from nuclear or fossil fuel sources. The use of renewables, and the range of options available when specifying energy from alternative sources, means that there isn't one certification or type of energy that is considered preferable. Fortunately, companies that use renewables are eager for the public to know about their environmental commitment and these products and services are almost always labeled or highlighted to consumers and purchasers.

PAPER PRODUCTION

Historically, paper production has been considered a dirty process that can negatively impact the environment at numerous points. However, in the last twenty years, governmental regulations, pressure from consumer and community groups, as well as investment by the industry itself has resulted in significant improvements to the environmental performance of many paper companies. Currently, areas of concern include water use, disposal of waste, energy sourcing, emissions, and the use of chlorine in paper production. Each mill deals with these issues differently and, in some cases, governmental regulations may prohibit the use of elemental chlorine and require mills to minimize any air and water pollution that is generated during paper production. However, energy conservation, sourcing from renewable sources, and the disposal of waste are rarely regulated. As energy has become more expensive, most mills have put conservation plans into place both for the sake of the bottom line and to minimize impact on the environment. Similarly, many mills have found ways to dispose of waste that include repurposing and reuse.

| PAPER PRODUCTION TARGET AREAS | FSC/ RECYCLED PULP FOR PRODUCTION | ELEMENTAL OR TOTALLY CHLORINE FREE | SOURCING OF RENEWABLE ENERGY | AIR & WATER SAFE PRODUCTION | SAFE & EQUITABLE WORK CONDITIONS |

Keeping up with all of the issues associated with paper production may be unrealistic for most designers, but paper companies do provide spec sheets that make it possible to compare one product with another. Printers may also provide information and advice about which companies produce products that have the least environmental impact.

RECYCLED PAPER

Every sheet of paper that is recycled prolongs the use of this highly disposable material and keeps material out of overflowing landfills. There has been some controversy about the benefits of recycling because of several negative environmental impacts associated with the de-inking of paper. However, most environmental organizations and independent studies conclude that the benefits of recycling outweigh the negatives.

Unfortunately, the labeling of paper containing recycled content varies tremendously and there are no formal regulations on what percentage of reclaimed material a sheet must contain in order to be called recycled. Therefore, it falls on the shoulders of consumers and distributors to make sense of confusing and sometimes misleading labeling.

When evaluating reclaimed paper, the most important distinction to make is between preconsumer and postconsumer waste.

Preconsumer waste refers to scraps and ends from the manufacturing process, as well as test sheets and overruns from printers that are collected and remanufactured into new paper.

Postconsumer waste refers to material that has reached the consumer, been used, and then collected to make new product. It is postconsumer waste that people commonly think of when they want recycled paper. However, preconsumer waste is reported to comprise 20 percent of the reclaimed content used in paper today. Copy paper often has some percentage (usually 10 to 30 percent) of recycled content, and unless otherwise specified, this labeling may simply indicate that mill waste is being fed back into the manufacturing process. While preconsumer waste is an important indication that mills are being efficient, it is vital that companies properly label products so consumers understand where reclaimed content comes from.

De-Inking

Generally paper can only be recycled up to six times. However, some countries' regulations and use of special inks have increased the number of times fiber can be used to nine. To achieve the bright white paper used for most printing projects, ink, adhesives, and other contaminants must be removed. As reclaimed material goes through the de-inking process, the natural wood fibers begin to break down and eventually only lower grades can be made from these shorter, weaker fibers. The exceptions are newsprint and cardboard, both of which can be produced with lower-quality reclaimed material that doesn't necessarily need to be de-inked. Even when reclaimed material does have to be whitened, it is usually done with hydrogen peroxide, which is considered to be much less harmful than the bleaching done with a chlorine derivative.

One of the main environmental concerns associated with the recycling process is sludge that consists of leftover materials from the de-inking process. Though some mills reprocess sludge for use as fertilizer, the practice is controversial because sludge and the resulting fertilizer often contain the heavy metals from ink. Since reclaimed material may have been printed before environmental regulations took effect, even materials that are banned for use today can show up in sludge. The safe collection and disposal of de-inking waste is an important environmental concern. However when paper is de-inked, any toxic elements found from sludge are less likely to contaminate groundwater supplies than if waste paper was sent directly to landfills.

PAPER FROM MIXED SOURCES

Since recycling results in the degradation of wood fibers, adding some percentage of virgin fiber to reclaimed material can prolong the use of weakened fibers. It is common to find environmentally friendly paper that is derived from mixed sources. To accommodate this trend, the FSC has created a certification for paper that uses some percentage of recycled content combined with virgin pulp from sustainably managed forests. One hundred percent postconsumer recycled paper may have a cost premium associated with

FSC CERTIFIED PULP + RECYCLED WASTE = MIXED SOURCES | BEST PRICE OPTION

Mixed Sources is a designation used for paper that combines virgin pulp from sustainably managed forests with recycled waste paper. Mixed source stocks can often represent the best price option when specing ecofriendly paper for production.

it because collecting and recycling waste paper is expensive and the demand is high. So using a sheet that is made with 20 to 40 percent postconsumer recycled waste with the remaining percentage coming from FSC certified sustainably managed virgin sources can provide the most cost-effective solution when specing ecofriendly paper.

TREE-FREE PAPER

Tree-free paper is made using materials not derived from wood fibers. Tree-free paper can be divided into two types: organic tree-free paper uses material derived from plant sources such as residues from agricultural crops or plants grown specifically for paper-making such as hemp, bamboo, and kenaf. Nonorganic tree-free paper is usually made of plastic polymers or minerals. Even though tree-free papers have been around for several decades, they have yet to capture a significant share of the paper market. It is important to note that some manufacturers consider any paper that uses no virgin fiber to be tree-free even though some products may actually contain a sizable amount of recycled wood fiber. Advocates for the use of alternative papers argue that tree-free paper is beneficial because these products save virgin trees. However, once the full lifecycle of individual products are analyzed, their environmental benefits are not always as impressive as they first seem. To date, the best option in tree-free paper is paper that is made from agricultural waste that would otherwise be thrown away or burned.

Organic Tree-Free Papers

Tree-free papers can provide an alternative to either recycled or virgin wood derived pulp. Even though some types of tree-free fibers (such as agricultural residues) can be produced with fewer chemicals, less energy, and less water than wood, the development of these materials for widespread consumer use has not yet occurred. In most cases, tree-free fiber is more expensive, not available in large quantities, and faces challenges in manufacturing because mills may have to be redesigned or retrofitted to accommodate the use of new materials in the papermaking process. Agricultural residues (including coffee, bananas, wheat, and rice residue) are considered the most preferable material to be used for paper production because these residues would otherwise go to waste.

Kenaf, hemp, and bamboo all grow in a matter of months rather than years and have been touted as wonder materials for paper production. However, the use of annual crops is complex and not advocated even by many environmental groups. Studies comparing the use of annual crops, such as kenaf or bamboo to tree plantations, do not necessarily support the substitution of these fibers for wood pulp. Annual crops may require more frequent doses of fertilizer and pesticides to produce the same amount of fiber and do not provide the secondary benefits of forests, including wildlife habitats, carbon trapping, and water-quality protection. The use of annual nontree derived fibers is still in its infancy and will require further investment and development before they become a viable alternative to tree pulp.

Nonorganic Tree-Free Papers

The future of nonorganic tree-free paper may lie in technological innovation and the development of new materials. Synthetic papers are smooth, come in different weights, take four-color process inks, and use limited or no wood or cotton fiber in their production. While technically recyclable, without special recycling facilities, items printed on synthetics may likely end up in landfills.

To date none of these applications are totally perfect, and some are considerably heavier than wood pulp paper. But these products do represent new opportunities for increased choice in environmentally preferable materials. They may one day prove that we really can invent our way out of the paper problem.

PRINTING

Working with a green printer or a printer that offers environmentally preferable production is one of the easiest ways for graphic designers to adopt sustainable practices. Choosing an established printer with a track record of a strong environmental commitment can eliminate the need for designers to do a lot of independent research on their own. Green printers may offer services that include offset litho, waterless litho, digital printing, as well as banner and signage services. In each case, a printer should stock a range of eco-friendly papers and other media at a variety of price points. When specing offset printing, choosing a company that offers a house sheet that combines postconsumer recycled content with FSC certified virgin fiber can be very cost effective and may even eliminate price premiums sometimes associated with green printing.

Key target areas to focus on when specing ecofriendly printing are paper procurement, reduction and disposal of waste (both paper and industrial chemicals), minimization of volatile organic compounds (VOCs) released, use of low volatile organic compounds vegetable oil–based ink, efficient use of materials, and energy sourcing and conservation. Any printer that advertises green or ecofriendly services should be able to provide both verbal and written descriptions of how each of these areas is being addressed. To quickly check how environmentally conscious your printer is, ask whether they have any third-party environmental certifications (ISO, FSC, etc). Unfortunately, certifications can be expensive for smaller companies and are only one option for evaluating a printer's performance and commitment to environmentally preferable processes and materials.

Offset lithography accounts for the vast majority of printed material that is produced and should be the first area of production targeted by graphic designers who want to improve their environmental footprints. It is a complicated process that may use toxic or unhealthy materials, it requires a great deal of energy, and it generates waste that must be properly disposed of. Fortunately, materials such as vegetable-based inks and citrus-based cleanup solutions as well as the use of processes such as waterless lithography can mitigate many of the negative effects of offset printing.

Green Printing Targets

ON-PRESS

| FSC OR RECYCLED PAPER STOCK | LOW VOC PRESS WASHES AND INKS | SOURCING OF RENEWABLE ENERGY | SAFE & EQUITABLE WORK CONDITIONS |

POSTPRODUCTION

| WATER-BASED GLUES & VARNISHES | SAFE DISPOSAL OF INKS & CHEMICALS | DISPOSAL & RECYCLING OF TRASH & PAPER |

Fast Steps To Greener Printing

WHAT YOU CAN DO:

- Use less paper by specifying lighter-weight paper, using both sides, and designing with standard sizes to get the most out of each sheet.

- Choose paper that is totally chlorine-free with high postconsumer recycled content or that is FSC certified.

- Avoid neon and metallic inks.

- Use water-based, nonchlorinated glues and coatings.

- Avoid printing more than you need.

- For small jobs, use digital printing.

- Specify the use of waterless lithography when possible.

WHAT YOUR PRINTER CAN DO:

- Use the most environmentally preferable inks and cleaners with low or no VOCs.

- Have programs in place to reduce water and energy use.

- Recycle as much as possible.

- Safely dispose of waste.

Inks and Washes

It is fairly common to hear soy inks being touted as an environmentally preferable option. Unfortunately, the benefits of soy are more hype than reality. The soy oil used in ink is similar to, and not any better than, ink made out of other vegetable-based materials (such as linseed or cottonseed oil) that have been in use for hundreds of years. Ink that is labeled soy is often less than 15 percent soy-based and some environmental organizations discourage buyers from specifying soy ink because soybeans are the crop most frequently planted in places where rainforests are cut and burned. In general, vegetable-based inks are better than inks that use petroleum (a nonrenewable resource) as a medium, however it is not necessary to specify soy in particular. Regardless of what kind of vegetable-based ink a printer may use, it is always prudent to ask what percentage of vegetable oil the ink includes since there are no regulations that stipulate a minimum percentage.

The most important environmental ramification of ink and other solutions used in offset lithography is the release of volatile organic compounds during the printing. VOCs are fumes emitted from solvents, inks, and cleaners used in the printing process. Prolonged exposure to VOCs can have negative effects on a person's health, and VOCs are a major contributor to ozone in the lower atmosphere. In recent years, companies have introduced products that have significantly reduced or even eliminated the VOCs emitted by inks, solvents, and press washes.

On the Horizon—Waterless Printing

Waterless printing offers significant advantages even when compared with other environmentally conscious offset printing methods. Unlike conventional offset lithography—a chemical process that requires water and dampening solutions—waterless printing uses a specific temperature range to transfer ink to the substrate. The elimination of water—and fountain solutions that contain isopropyl alcohol or their substitutes—vastly reduces the amount of water used and VOCs emitted on press. Waterless printing is also more efficient; printers that have switched to waterless printing report increased productivity of more than 100 percent. Unfortunately, so few printers offer this service that there is a great deal of misunderstanding about the technology. The truth is that waterless is cost effective and can be used to produce everything that would be printed with traditional offset lithography.

Digital Printing

Digital printing is usually considered environmentally preferable for jobs requiring fewer than 2,000 copies. It is also a good option for larger pieces such as signage or banners. Digital printing includes toner-based printers such as laser printers, which use heat to adhere dry pigment to paper, as well as ink-jet systems, which spray water and solvent-based ink directly onto paper or other printing material. Digital printing is environmentally preferable because toner inks don't use any alcohol or emit VOCs, and even ink-jet printing has virtually eliminated off-gassing.

One of the main benefits of digital printing is that it doesn't require messy cleanup. Some companies have programs that allow used ink cartridges and other printing waste (such as printer components and used ink depositories) to be returned to the manufacturer for recycling. In the case of ink-jet printing, there are new environmentally friendly papers, manmade and natural, that can be run in both small and wide-format printers.

GUIDE TO ENVIRONMENTALLY FRIENDLY PAPERS

The following chart shows brands and sheets of paper that have made an effort to decrease their negative impact on the environment. These are only a small sampling of companies and products that are available. If you have a preferred vendor, it is likely that they carry some FSC certified and/or PCW recycled paper. Comparing products from different companies can help consumers choose the best paper for their job and assess specific environmental and social targets.

	Color Finishes	Brightness	Printing	FSC Certified	Recycled (PCW)	Carbon Neutral Green Power	Elemental Chlorine Free
CASCADES ROLLAND ENVIRO100 PRINTMATTE	Smooth Opaque		Offset	Yes	100%	Biomass Renewable	Most costly option. Requires more production time. Requires signatures.
COSTA RICA NATURAL PAPER BANANA	Textured	Colored	Digital Offset	No	5–15% Banana Fiber 85–95% PCW	No	Process Chlorine Free
DOMTAR EARTHCOTE	White Gloss Matte	White 84 GE	Offset	Yes	30% PCW	No	No
DOMTAR OPAQUE PLAINFIELD	White 3 Colors Smooth Vellum	96 GE	Copier Digital Offset Ink-Jet	Yes	None	No	No
DOMTAR EARTH CHOICE OFFICE PAPER	White Smooth	92 GE	Laser Copier DI Presses Ink-Jet	Yes	None	No	No
FRENCH PAPER DUR-O-TONE	White Colors		Offset	No	100%	Yes Hydro Powered	Process Chlorine Free
FOX RIVER EVERGREEN	Balanced White Soft White		Offset	Yes	50% PCW 50% Bamboo	Yes	Elemental Chlorine Free PCW is Process Chlorine Free
GILBERT PAPER GILBERT COTTON	Pure Ultra White Cotton Cream	Cockle Finish	Offset Recycled is Laser Ink-Jet Ready	No	100% Cotton Fibers or 100% PCW Cotton	Yes	Elemental Chlorine Free
MOHAWK STRATHMORE SCRIPT	Colors White	96 Bright	Digital Offset	Yes	30% PCW	Wind Power	No

	Color Finishes	Brightness	Printing	FSC Certified	Recycled (PCW)	Carbon Neutral Green Power	Chlorine Free
MOHAWK OPTIONS	Crystal White Marble White	96 Bright	Digital Offset	Yes	30% PCW	Wind Power	No
MOHAWK BECKETT CONCEPT	White/ Vellum Finish/ Colors	98 Bright	Electric and Web Offset	Yes	100% PCW	Yes and Green Seal Certified	No
NEENAH CLASSIC CREST COVER	White	96 White	Offset	Yes	100% PCW	Yes and Green e Certified Carbon Neutral	No
NEENAH STARWHITE	White		Offset	Yes 100% FSC Virgin Fiber	NA	Yes and Green e Certified Carbon Neutral	No
NEENAH CLASSIC LAID COVER	White	89 White	Offset	Yes	100% PCW	Yes and Green e Certified Carbon Neutral	No
NEW LEAF REINCARNATION MATTE	White	90 White	Offset	No	50% PCW with 100% recycled content	Yes Green e Certified	Process Chlorine Free
NEW LEAF SYMPHONY SILK COATED	White Three Finishes	90 White	Offset	Yes	30% PCW	No	Elemental Chlorine Free
NEW LEAF OPAQUE SMOOTH	White	88 White	Offset	Yes	100% PCW	Yes and Green e Certified Bio-Mass Energy & Wind Power	Process Chlorine Free
SAPPI FINE PAPER MCCOY	White	96	Offset	Yes	10% PCW	Yes and 100% Green e Certified Renewable Energy	No
SAPPI FINE PAPER TRIPLE GREEN	White		Offset	Some % Request Detail	No; Locally sourced sugar cane fiber	No	Elemental Chlorine Free
SMART PAPER KNIGHTKOTE MATTE	White		Offset	No	30% PCW 50% total recycled content	No	Elemental Chlorine Free

Chapter 15:
User Experience and User Interface Design

USER EXPERIENCE (UX) DESIGN

UX design studies how users feel about an experience. UX designers typically evaluate an experience's ease of use, perceived value, and how efficiently a user completed various tasks throughout the entire experience. User experience evolved from the user centric design philosophy—a philosophy focused on making design decisions that are rooted in the needs and desires of users. Many design disciplines can be included under the UX umbrella, including user interface design.

USER INTERFACE DESIGN

Within the practice of UX design, user interface (UI) design is typically a combination between interaction design and visual design. Simply put, a user interface provides the tools ('interface') for the user to get through an on-line experience. The user interface design process has different phases, each with different activities.

- User research (Discovery)
- Sketching/wireframing/prototyping (Design)
- Visual design (Design)
- Usability testing (Design)
- User interface development (Development)

A designer, information architect and a user interface developer (i.e., front-end developer) will typically own a particular piece of the user interface design process. In smaller organizations one person might be responsible for all activities within of the user interface design, while in a larger organization there might be one person responsible for every task.

User Research

User research is a key component of the user interface design process and is the main driver of the discovery phase. User research encompasses many different investigative methods to gain a deeper understanding of the problems, and needs, of potential users. User research occurs during both the discovery and design phases.

Ethnographic Research: A qualitative research method that studies people and how they work in a natural environment. Rather than asking target questions in a survey, ethnographic research requires a researcher to visit and watch people in an environment where the interface will be used. The primary benefit to ethnographic research is that uncovers underlying and previously unnoticed problems.

Focus Groups: A moderated discussion with a group of demographically similar individuals, who are considered potential users of a product. Specifically, focus groups give designers an opportunity to learn more about the target audiences' thoughts and decision-making process. A focus group can help uncover general trends on how valuable a potential solution could be.

User Interviews: Face-to-face discussions, typically with current users, or someone who is likely to be a user. These interviews are typically focused on 5–7 key topics. The interviewer is usually a designer or product manager. The conversation is designed to be open ended, with the interviewer guiding the discussion. In most interviews the goal is to dive deep into a few topics to help surface existing problems or reveal new ones.

Sketching

A sketch is a fast and easy way to layout an initial user interface idea. The low fidelity nature of a sketch allows for a quick, visual articulation of thoughts, an increased number of potential solutions, and a opportunity for non-designers to participate in the design process. A sketch will force a designer to think about, and prioritize, the content and objectives of a particular and can help discover problems earlier in the process.

Sketching Tools

- Pen and paper
- Whiteboard and dry-erase markers

Wireframing

Wireframes in Web design are similar to a blueprint in architectural design. It provides all the details on structure, content, and functionality prior to the visual design of a user interface. A wireframe will define what goes on a page, where it goes, and why it goes there without having to worry about elements such as font and colors. Wireframes won't outline every single page, instead key templates will be developed. The templates created will be used to extrapolate the rest of the experience.

Wireframes are meant to be shared, dissected, and iterated upon. Because wireframes are completed early in the process, designers have more freedom to make mistakes, learn, and make changes without incurring high cost for change.

- Prior to starting wireframes, designers should have a clear understanding of the products, users, and their goals, and a clear grasp of the projects business goals.

- Work in actual pixel dimensions

- Don't use fonts that can't be used on the Web

- Work in a grid (Chapter 6.)

- Be consistent in page numbering

- Track revisions

WIREFRAMING TOOLS

Visio (Windows): http://office.microsoft.com/en-us/visio/

Omnigraffle (Mac): www.omnigroup.com/products/omnigraffle/

Blasmiq: www.balsamiq.com/

Adobe Fireworks: www.adobe.com/products/fireworks.html

Mockflow: www.mockflow.com/

Protoshare: www.protoshare.com/

Prototyping

Prototypes are built by linking multiple wireframes together, through hotspots on a page, to simulate a particular experience. Typically the experience in a prototype is simplified from the full experience, but provides enough interaction to learn how a user will behave. Because of their simplistic nature, prototypes are a great tool to use during usability testing sessions.

BENEFITS OF PROTOTYPING

- Prototypes are tangible and offer users something to interact with.

- The in-process nature of a prototype encourages users and stakeholders to provide feedback without having to worry about hurting someone's feelings.

- Prototypes are a clearer deliverable to business stakeholders or clients.

- A prototype can quickly reveal design problems, particularly those which were never considered.

Blasmiq: www.balsamiq.com/

Adobe Fireworks: www.adobe.com/products/fireworks.html

Invision: www.invisionapp.com/

Fieldtest: http://fieldtestapp.com/

Usability Testing
Usability testing is a technique used during the design phase and helps evaluate the usefulness with potential users. Usability testing is a method of user research typically occurring after an artifact (i.e., a wireframe or visual design comp) has been created. Usability testing is conducted by a designer—in a controlled setting—with a specific set of goals that need to be accomplished.

5 TRUTHS ABOUT USABILITY TESTING

Reminds designers that they aren't the user: Usability testing will remind people that different people can interpret the same experience very differently, and often the people testing the site do not think the same way a designer thinks.

Testing a little is always better than not testing: Even if a design is tested with one user, it's better than not testing at all. Usability testing, even with just one person, can reveal previously unseen problems with an experience.

Test early, test often: The more a design is tested, and the earlier it gets tested, the sooner a designer can gain insight and make adjustments to the experience.

Testing helps inform a decision: Testing a design will yield priceless insight. The insight, combined with the experience and judgment of a designer, will help designers and stakeholders make more informed decisions about a particular experience.

Reaction from a real user trumps everything: No amount of research, data, or design knowledge will ensure that a given design will be successful. Until people actually use the website, everything is based on thoughts and assumptions. User feedback gained during a usability session will help improve even the most well-intentioned experiences by validating some design decisions and by pointing out areas where the design must be improved.

User Interface Development
To create a working user interface a front-end (user interface) developer uses the visual design as construction plan to build the actual experience in code. The constructed user interface will support the exchange of information by giving the user a way, via the interface, to interact with back-end processes and databases.

HTML (HyperText Markup Language): This is the most common language used in Web design. HTML is made up of tags or directions that specify how a Web page should be displayed in a browser. HTML is primarily concerned with presentation, structure, and linking rather than programming. HTML documents may also include JavaScript, CSS, and other coding languages.

The most recent version of HTML is HTML 5. While HTML 5 is still under development, its primary goal is to improve the language so that it better supports the latest multimedia while keeping the language easily understood by humans, computers and other devices. Combined with CSS3 and Java script, HTML 5 allows for more advance design options, particularly typography, advance graphics, animations, and transitions. Many features of HTML5 have been built with the consideration of being able to run on low-powered devices such as smartphones and tablets.

CSS (Cascading Style Sheets): This is a method for controlling styling and formatting of HTML pages. It can be applied across multiple documents.

Java: A scripting language created by Sun Microsystems that can be used to create Web applications.

AJAX: Also known as Asynchronous JavaScript and XML, AJAX is a method of building interactive applications for the Web that process user requests immediately. This combination of techniques and programming achieves better interactivity mostly by transferring small amounts of data at a time so that entire Web pages don't need to be reloaded each time a small action is performed.

MOBILE UI DESIGN CONSIDERATIONS

In recent years, the advent of the smartphone has pushed mobile UX into the forefront of design. No longer will people visit a mobile site, or download an app, for the novelty of the experience. Today's mobile users won't tolerate bad user experiences. Although the same design methods and processes used for developing desktop/laptop experiences can be used for mobile experiences, it's important to remember "Don't shrink, rethink (coined by Nokia)".

Tips for Mobile Design
- Prioritize and feature key functionality from the desktop/laptop experience.
- Offer mobile-only functionality when it makes sense (e.g., give users the ability to scan barcodes when visiting their favorite retail store.)
- Navigation and content exploration is completed though touch. Because the finger isn't as precise as a mouse, larger click targets may be needed

- Speed of page loading is critical regardless of how a user is accessing the content (computer, tablet, smartphone), but speed becomes more important on a mobile device. Simplifying the site structure and content can help increase speed.
- Mobile devices offer more opportunities for distraction. Make the experience efficient as possible by simplifying the experience.

User Responsive Design and Mobile
Responsive design is an approach where a website automatically responds to the environment and behavior of a user to present a website's images, text, and navigation in the most appropriate manner. The flexibility of responsive design is supported through the use of flexible grids and layouts, images, and CSS media queries. Practicing smart design eliminates the need to design multiple experiences to support desktops, laptops, iPads, iPhones, etc.

Recommended Reading
Sketching User Experience
Buxton, Bill
Elsevier, 2007

Smashing UX Design
Allen, Jesmond; Chudley, James
John Wiley & Sons, Ltd, 2012

The Handbook of Global User Research
Schumacher, Robert M.
Elsevier, 2010

Designing Interactions
Moggridge, Bill
MIT Press, 2007

Web Hosting Companies
www.inmotionhosting.com
www.webhostinghub.com
www.arvixe.com

Chapter 16: Standard Forms and Contracts

(excerpted from Managing the Design Process books by Terry Lee Stone)

CREATIVE BRIEFS ARE STRATEGIC TOOLS

Computer scientists have a saying, "Garbage in, garbage out." It means that computers can process a lot of data output, but it will only be as good as the information that was put into the system. It's pretty much the same in design. When creative is developed from great client input, the results can be great. If not, well, it's a recipe for falling short of the mark. Without a well-identified and articulated set of objectives and goals that is rooted in thorough background and research information, a design can't grow out of a solid foundation. There needs to be a summary of all the factors that can impact a design project. It is well worth the time it takes to develop it.

What's in a Creative Brief?

In the best cases, a creative brief is created through meetings, interviews, readings, and discussions between a client and designer. It should contain background information, target audience details, information on competitors, short- and long-term goals, and specific project details. A creative brief will answer these questions:

- What is this project?
- Who is it for?
- Why are we doing it?
- What needs to be done? By whom? By when?
- Where and how will it be used?

Without making a framework for the project, the designer won't be able to understand the parameters or context that needs to be worked within. The creative brief provides an objective strategic tool that can be agreed and acted upon. It can serve as a set of metrics by which to judge and evaluate the appropriateness of a design. At the very least, all the relevant project information is contained within a single document that can be shared as guidelines for the entire client and designer project team.

Negative Impact of No Creative Brief

Any designer who simply launches into a design assignment without a proper briefing doesn't have all the relevant facts and opinions to do a well-informed job. They are also asking for trouble as work progresses. Approvals come with buy in; buy in is so often a result of feeling included and asked for input. Sure, the odds are that they can design something interesting and eye-appealing based on their gut instincts, but these solutions are not grounded in solid understanding, and they are more easily dismissed by both clients and target audiences.

How to Do a Creative Brief

- Develop a list of questions for a client that will provide you with the information you need to proceed with the design.

- Ask the client to identify a list of people in their organization who should participate in the briefing process.

- Do client interview session(s). Meet the selected people one on one for more candid responses. Send clients the questions in advance so that they are better prepared to respond.

- Take notes and/or record the interviews. Having two design team members on hand works better than doing it alone, because it allows the conversation to keep flowing, while still being recorded. Do remember that recording someone without their permission is inappropriate and illegal.

- Compile and analyze the interview findings. Create a summary document. Where is there consensus? Where are the overlaps and tangents?

- Write the creative brief. Include the essential items listed on pages 142–143, and format the document to be easy for both you and the client to use.

- Send the creative brief to the client for approval. Some designers do a design criteria document (see page 146) instead of sending the actual creative brief, which they share only with the design team. Whichever the document, send a summary of findings to the client first before any design begins.

- With client approval, distribute the creative brief to the design team. Some firms do this in a kick-off meeting; others just provide a document. Either way, this is the design team briefing. The creative brief works as the guiding framework and background document to inform all design development.

- Both the client and the design team members should evaluate all design solutions based upon the creative brief. Learn more about evaluating design on pages 164–165.

The 10 Most Important Things to Include in a Creative Brief

1

2

3

4

5

Background Summary. Who is the client? What is the product or service? What are the strengths, weaknesses, opportunities, and threats, or SWOT. Research, reports, and any otherdocuments that help you understand the situation.

Overview. What is the project? What are we designing and why? Why do we need this project? What's the opportunity?

Drivers. What is our goal for this project? What are we trying to achieve? What is the purpose of our work? What are our top three objectives?

Audience. Who are we talking to? What do they think of us? Why should they care?

Competitors. Who is the competition? What are they telling the audience that we should be telling them? SWOT analysis on them? What differentiates us from them?

6

Tone.
How should we be communicating? What adjectives describe the feeling or approach?

7

Message.
What are we saying with this piece exactly? Are the words already developed or do we need to develop them? What do we want audiences to take away?

8

Visuals.
Are we developing new images or picking up existing ones? If we are creating them, who, what, where are we shooting? And why?

9

Details.
Any mandatory info? List of deliverables? Preconceived ideas? Format parameters? Limitations and restrictions? Timeline, schedule, budget?

10

People.
Who are we reporting to? Who exactly is approving this work? Who needs to be informed of our progress? By what means?

Managing to a Creative Brief

A creative brief is used not only at the start of a project, but throughout the entire design process. It is the one constant element that has been agreed upon and is objective enough to act as a guideline. Clients primarily use it to get organized, and to develop consensus within their own enterprises. They then use it to determine if the design actually solves the problem it was intended to. Designers use creative briefs to fact-find and understand their client, building knowledge about both perception and reality of the problem at hand. Designers often find out that what their client thinks is the problem is not the problem at all. These are the things that become revealed in the briefing.

Once the creative brief is agreed upon by both the designer and client, it is a useful tool for getting all members of the design team on board and ready to work on the project. The designers have relevant grounding to inform their thinking, the copywriter has messaging information, the production and project managers have milestones and due dates, and the account executive has met and bonded with all client stakeholders. Everyone has what they need to work, no matter what their responsibility is.

Creative Briefs vs. Design Criteria

Sometimes, designers take the extra step of translating a creative brief provided by their clients into a design criteria. If a creative brief is a tool that provides a framework and roadmap for a design project, the design criteria is the summary of the approach and a preplan for the creative. The design criteria describes what the designer will do to solve the problem—i.e., the creative strategy.

Taking the time to develop design criteria is very important if the client is contradictory or indecisive. It gives the designers another opportunity to clarify details before they begin creative work by team members who tend to be the most highly skilled and most expensive in terms of hourly rate. It creates a sureness that designer and client are in agreement.

Who Uses a Creative Brief?

Both the client and the design team use the creative brief. Creating it helps a client crystallize the salient information, gather their thoughts, and research and identify goals and objectives. It provides an opportunity for all stakeholders to give input and have their say. It aids in client buy in of the resulting designs mostly because the client team has all provided input.

For the designer, the brief provides relevant information to alleviate guesswork. Who knows the client's business better than the client? By gathering this information concisely in one document, the creative brief is a criteria for evaluation, outlining metrics that indicate success, and ultimately holding the designer accountable—unless of course, the designer can convince their client that the creative brief is wrong.

Designer

- Provides background and foundation for design.
- Uncovers hidden truths and apparent insights.
- Reveals personality and values of client as an organization and as individuals.
- Aids in buy in because client has had their say.
- Becomes the justification for all designs presented
- Concisely informs all members of the team.
- Provides criteria for evaluation.
- Helps aid against off-target creative and scope creep.

Value of a Creative Brief

Client

- Clarifies goals and objectives
- Articulates facts and assumptions
- Opportunity for all stakeholders to provide input.
- Builds consensus.
- Provides criteria for evaluation.
- Holds the designer accountable.
- Indicates metrics for success.

Budgeting for Design

A lot of designers think money is a main reason they win or lose a client's business. They are often right. Pricing work properly is a skill acquired through practice. It takes a keen instinct for what the marketplace will pay and what the design firm will need.

How the work is priced is only one factor in getting a design job from a client. Other factors from the client's perspective include

- *Relevant Experience:* Has the designer worked on a similar project in the past? What does it look like? What are the results of the design?

- *Right Attitude:* Is the designer enthusiastic and eager to begin work on the project?

- *Good Chemistry:* Does it seem like a good fit? Does the designer "get us"? Do we like the designer as a person?

- *Portfolio/Style:* Is the designer's work appealing? Does it have a discernible style that meshes with our needs? Is the designer creative enough?

- *Perceived Reliability:* Did the designer show up on time? Do we think we can trust the designer? (Since the client is sometimes meeting the designer for the first time, this is often subjective.)

- *A Referral:* Did someone we know and trust refer this designer to us? Did the designer get a good recommendation?

- *Luck:* Is the designer in the right place at the right time?

It is arguable which comes first—creating a schedule or creating a budget. Sometimes a client just tells the designer how much money they have for a particular project. Usually, though, the client requests a price from the designer. The designer's compensation is an essential element in a designer–client agreement.

Pricing is what you tell the client it will cost for the project. This includes fees (your compensation) and expenses (reimbursable outside costs for items purchased for the project). Budgeting is how you appropriate and manage these fees and expenses. In this chapter, we'll look at money in both ways.

Here are some key factors to consider when pricing a design job:

- *Scope of Work*
  What exactly are we doing? What services are we providing?
  What are the deliverables? In what format?

- *Resources*
  Who will do the work? Do we have to supplement our team with additional designers? With what skills? How much do they cost? Do we need our senior or junior designers to do the work?

- *Scheduling*
  How much time do we have? How much time do we need?
  How much time does each team member need? Do we need to juggle several projects simultaneously? How does that affect us?

- *The Client*
  Have we worked for this client before? Are they decisive or prone to revisions? Are there layers of management that must be appeased or is there one decision maker? How available is that person?

- *Collaborators*
  Beyond designers, who else needs to work on this project?
  What will they do? What will it cost? How much will be provided directly by the client?

- *Quality*
  What are the client's expectations? Are they willing to pay for it? Have we done something like this before? Will there be a lot of research, or can we immediately get to work?

- *Expertise*
  Do we have it? How steep is the learning curve if we don't?
  How will we know when we have a great design for this client?

- *Cash Flow*
  What other jobs are in-house right now? How much money do we need? Design is a business, and all businesses have real financial requirements and obligations. What are ours?

The answers to these questions have cost implications. The more experienced a design manager is at answering and anticipating these tough questions and the better his or her documented records are on previous projects, the more accurate the design manager will be in pricing and budgeting projects.

Determine Your Rate
You can determine an hourly rate for design services in several ways. Many design organizations worldwide have published this kind of information as a reference. For example, in the United States, the AIGA publishes an annual wage and salary survey. You can divide the average annual salary reported in the survey by the number of billable hours in a year (1,500 hours is a good round-number average to use). This calculation gives you an hourly rate based on the organization's member submission information. A discussion with peers and colleagues may yield a ballpark idea of what they charge per hour. However, many people shy away from this kind of conversation and often don't tell the truth. If they trust you, and don't directly compete with you for client business, they may reveal this information.

Calculation Based on Real Needs
Here is a formula for determining your hourly rate based on your actual costs of staying in business.

It's not the only way to determine an hourly rate, and it doesn't factor in the value of the work to a client's business or a premium for your expertise; it's merely based on actual economic needs.

Reviewing Pricing
Designers must know their hourly rate to set their fee for particular design jobs—both the breakeven hourly rate to understand the lowest fee they should charge, and the published hourly rate to allow for profit and tax obligations (see page 95). Calculating a fee using both sets of rates shows you where the job must be priced (breakeven) and what is an optimum price (published hourly rate). However, it is hard to know exactly how many hours it will take to do any design project. Therefore, any estimate based on hours is just that: an educated guess on the duration and complexity of the work. As such, pricing jobs strictly on hourly rates is not a 100 percent accurate approach.

Evaluating Your Calculations
To get a more well-rounded view of pricing, review the project total you calculated using your published hourly rate and ask yourself the following questions: Does this total reflect the value of this work to the client? Does it reflect the expertise we bring to the project?

Can we get more money for this job based on who the client is? In other words, is this client a small regional startup company or a well-funded multinational corporation? Little businesses typically have little budget, and big businesses should have a big budget. What have we charged for similar projects in the past? How is this project the same or different from those? Is that reflected in this price calculation?

What do we think our competitors would charge for this project? Why do we think that? Can we discuss our calculation with anyone?

(Talking about pricing design with a colleague or two is fine. Note, however, that in most countries, banding together as a profession and determining an industrywide price is illegal. It's a form of collusion called price-fixing. This is why design organizations as a group rarely discuss in public or publish pricing information.)

Is there any published information on pricing for this type of work? For example, the Graphic Artist Guild's Pricing and Ethical Guidelines publishes rate information. The organization polls its members, has them price certain kinds of projects, and then publishes that information. It can legally do this in the United States because it is a trade union, and it operates under different laws than nonprofit design (arts) organizations.

Does this price calculation seem high or low based on your gut instinct? How should it be adjusted?

Learning about Pricing

Two design firms can have the same published hourly rate and calculate two different project fees using that rate. For example, one design firm may work slower or have more people involved; this means it estimates more hours into a project and it charges more. Only by keeping very good records, especially time sheets, on all projects and then comparing estimates to actual costs can designers price their work accurately over time.

A trusted client may be candid and tell the designer what competitors would charge on a particular job, particularly if the designer lost the job to a competitor. It's important to learn why a design firm lost out on an opportunity, but remember that it isn't always a question of money.

Another useful strategy is to develop relationships with other designers that can include discussions of money.

Remember that big fees don't necessarily mean big profits. It all comes down to how the project is run. How long did the designer work on the project to earn that fee? Maybe we spent very little time on the project, but the work was tremendously valuable to the client's business. These things are unique to every design project. It is why most designers are always wondering whether they charged enough on a job and whether they could have made more money.

Clients and Money

Not all designers are driven by money. Scores of designers are much more interested in the artistic than the financial aspects of design. However, all designers need money to survive.

Reframing financial negotiations with clients means designers must be fully engaged in an active conversation with the client. They need to be confident about their ability to use design to meet their client's business goals; believe in the value of their work; and be willing to ask for fair compensation. Money often coincides with issues of self-worth, so you must believe in yourself and your abilities as a designer before negotiating fees in order to achieve the best outcome financially and creatively.

Tips for Dealing with Clients About Money

· Be clear. What exactly does the price include?

· Define payment terms. When do you expect to be paid? Upon completion? Within thirty days?

· Stick to the fee. If you must raise the fee, explain the increase in a change order.

· State the number of revisions and stick to them. Note any exceptions or additions in a change order.

· Keep good records. Provide time sheets and expense receipts as a backup to your billing if the client requests it.

- Integrate the schedule with regular cost reviews. Review these frequently, and communicate any problems or issues. Alert the client. Make sure you capture all time (e.g., telephone consultation, travel time, etc.).

- Don't surprise the client. To get paid quickly, make your invoices match your estimates exactly.

- Keep fees consistent. Base fees on a rate the client understands. No fire sales, no discounts, no arbitrary changes in pricing structure.

- Get it in writing. Have anything related to money signed by the client, for legal reasons and to prompt a detailed conversation about money before any work gets underway.

- Get all related client paperwork and financial information. Get a purchase order number if it's required. Include a vendor number on your invoices if you were assigned one. Introduce yourself to the contact person in accounts payable.

- Stay in communication. Do this throughout the process, with the client contact and the accounting department, if necessary

- Consider incentives. This can be a discount for prompt or fast payment of invoices, or a late fee as a penalty for slow-paying clients.

Questions for Negotiating
Sometimes, a client can't afford your fee. The question is: what is actually happening? Investigate further:

- Will they ever be able to afford it or is it a temporary problem?

- Do they want to work with you?

- Can the scope to reduce deliverables be narrowed?

- Can they provide you with referrals?

- Will you get a great portfolio piece?

- Will you gain recognition, credibility, or some other benefit besides money?

- Is it worth taking the job?

Sometimes, you may wish to negotiate pricing. Naturally, it needs to be in your best interest to do so. Here are some questions to ask:

- Can we have longer to work on the project, perhaps fitting this job in between other work?

- Will the project challenge us creatively and open new doors?

- Can we do research and learn new skills that are marketable to other clients by doing this job?

- Will we have a chance to work with some exciting new collaborators in brand new ways?

These factors may be interesting enough to you to make it worth dropping your prices to get the job.

Talking Revisions

Communicating with clients about revisions is a huge part of managing client expectations regarding money. The best strategy is to be clear in the designer–client agreement about how many revisions are included. That way, the client understands the meaning of revision and round of revisions, and when they will start receiving additional charges because of those changes.

For more information, see page 40–41.

Even with this clearly spelled out, many designers are unsure how to corral their client and alert them that they have exceeded the planned scope and revision allotment, for fear of losing the client. If the client has agreed to the terms in the designer–client agreement, it is okay to bill them. Just let them know what is happening in a professional manner.

Too often, designers are afraid to ask for additional compensation for additional work.

This makes it harder for the industry to be treated fairly in this aspect of the business. When you practice without fair compensation, including receiving additional fees for additional work, you are hurting not only yourself, but all designers everywhere.

Designer Fault

Some designers hesitate to charge for revisions because they feel they caused the revisions. This may be true. An evaluation will reveal the cause(s) of a revision in a design project. If it is poor performance on the designer's part, the designer should not charge it to the client.

Ballpark Estimate:

This is an initial rough estimate based on high-level client objectives, with a large margin for uncertainty. The deliverables, scope of work, and corresponding resource requirements may not be clear yet, so out of necessity, the estimate must allow for these things. Typically, a price range, rather than a fixed fee is stated.

Budgetary Estimate:

This is a more accurate view of project-related costs based on a much clearer scope of work. It is contingent on a fairly accurate view of the work to be done, which still may be in a state of flux. As such, conditions and parameters should be stated—for example, "This estimate is based on available information, and will be reviewed based on approved design concept."

Definitive Estimate:
This is a time-consuming and detailed estimate created once the full scope of work, final deliverables, and detailed work flow are known. A full work breakdown structure (see page 66) is completed, the project is scheduled, and the team is assembled before the estimate is prepared.

Eight Payment Strategies
Designers can be compensated for their work by way of a variety of payment methods. Clients and designers should negotiate a payment strategy that meets both of their needs. Here are some interesting options:

1. Fixed Fee
Agree to a total fee for the project. Invoice 50 percent before work begins and 50 percent upon completion. Bill expenses at the end of the project. This is a good strategy for smaller projects with clear deliverables.

2. Progress Payment
A project is broken down into sequential phases of work, with the fees and, possibly, expenses invoiced at the completion of each phase. Related to this is dividing an agreed-upon project fee into monthly installments. These progress payments are based on the calendar, and not the work completed, as is the case with the phased approach.

3. Modular
Divide a large project into smaller modules of work and bill them as separate jobs. This works well for related but not sequential work. For example, design a company's corporate identity in January, and then do the website in June.

4. Retainer
In this ongoing designer–client relationship, the designer agrees to a fixed fee, typically invoiced monthly, for a specific amount of work. This strategy is good for ongoing publications or clearly defined repetitive tasks—for example, developing a new top page for a website every week.

5. Hourly
In this open-ended agreement, the client pays the designer a fixed hourly rate for every hour worked on a project. Good recordkeeping is essential here. Some clients ask for a not-to-exceed ceiling on hours prior to commencement of work to stay within a certain budget.

6. Deferred
The designer and client negotiate a fee, but payment is deferred until a mutually agreed-upon date. This is somewhat risky for the designer, but good for a client with a startup business. Perhaps the fee negotiated is slightly higher than normal to offset the risk.

7. Profit Participation

The designer agrees to be paid a certain fee, typically lower than his or her standard practice, but in addition receives profit participation in the client's business. This ties design effectiveness to sales and business results and is another good strategy for startup clients or new products the designer is intricately involved in creating.

8. Trade

The designer is paid in-kind with client services or products instead of with money. Such barter agreements work if a clear value for the designer's work is established. Make sure the design is traded for the wholesale (not retail) value of the client's service or product.

Rights and Compensation

One thing designers must consider in terms of money and design is ownership of the work being created. Who owns what, and how the work may or may not be used, is a negotiating point that also has financial implications. This concept is tied to the designer's intellectual property rights and the client's right to use the work they commissioned the designer to create.

Intellectual property

Intellectual property (a legal reference to the creations of the mind: inventions, literary and artistic works, etc.) is debated by lawyers worldwide. In the United States and Canada, for example, all creative work is owned by its creator until the creator transfers ownership in writing to someone else. This is the cornerstone of copyright protection (legal protection that gives the creator of an original work exclusive rights to use that work within a certain period). Other countries may take different views and have different laws, so designers must understand what is true and legal in the country in which they practice design.

There are some complex rights and usage agreements that can affect a graphic designer. For example, in the United States many clients require designers to work under a work-for-hire contract, which is a written (not verbal) legal agreement between the designer and client stating that the client owns all work developed by the designer under the contract. In essence, it legally makes the client the creator of the work and affords them all the related rights of a creator. This isn't a bad thing, but it means the client is now undisputedly the owner of the work. As such, a designer might want additional compensation.

It is important that the designer and client know who owns the work and how it may be used. For example, when a client owns outright an illustration that a designer developed for a pamphlet, the client can use that image in any future advertisement or on their web page, without paying the designer anything additional. Therefore, a designer would want to charge more for this kind of complete transfer of rights and ownership. Alternatively, it could be a negotiating point: Charge a lower fee, but the client has restricted usage rights for the work.

Compensation and the notion of intellectual property is a good topic for a designer to discuss with an attorney. You can also seek information from various design organizations, and share this information with your peers. Know your rights, know your client's needs, and know the laws at the intersection of these two things.

Factors to consider when thinking about the material worth of usage rights and your corresponding fee for a design include

- The value placed on similar work (perhaps even for other clients)

- The category or media in which the work will be used

- The geographic location or area of distribution for the work

- How the client will use the work (for what purpose)

- How long the work will be used

- How many items will be produced that incorporate the work

Licensing Options

Most of the work graphic designers do will be commissioned by a client for a mutually agreed upon sum or fixed project fee. However, some designers license their work to clients instead. Licensing means allowing or granting use of an original work for varied compensation based on the license. Usually, licensing takes one of these two forms in design:

Use-based Licensing

The designer's compensation is based on how the work is used.

- This often occurs for images such as illustration and photography.

- It's frequently negotiated for publications, print or digital.

- Additional uses, or changes in use, require additional agreements and compensation to the designer.

- Payment by the licensee (client) is typically made to the licensor (designer) before the work is used.

Royalty-based Licensing

The designer's compensation is a royalty or a percentage of the money received from the net sales of a product that incorporates the designer's work.

- This often occurs for merchandise for sale.

- It's frequently negotiated by product designers.

- Compensation is tied to sales and the public's acceptance of the product.

- The licensee (client) must allow the licensor (designer) to review accounting/product sales records.

- Payments typically are made quarterly, but can be negotiated otherwise.

- An advance on royalties is a payment the licensee (client) makes to the licensor (designer) upfront that is then deducted from the royalties to be paid in the future.

Even if you do not choose to be paid under a licensing agreement, your subcontractors may prefer to be paid this way. For example, it is common for an illustrator to allow his or her work to be utilized through a use-based licensing agreement.

○ Glossary

A

A sheets: ISO paper sizes based on metric dimensions. The ISO standard is used everywhere except North America for determining standard trim sizes.

Accordion fold: Zigzag type of fold in a sheet of paper where two or more parallel folds open in the manner of an accordion, permitting the paper to be extended to its full breadth with a single pull. Also called a *fan fold*.

Agricultural fibers: Fiber harvested from tree-free organic sources that are grown specifically for use in paper production and often bearing the label "tree-free."

Agricultural residues: Fibers recovered from annual crops usually planted as food crops or for commercial use (such as corn, sugar cane, and wheat) that is used to make paper.

Aqueous coating: A water-based coating that is applied at the end of a press run to protect a printed piece against moisture, dirt, and scuffing.

Asymmetry: Elements that when placed on opposite sides of a page, line, or plane are not symmetrical.

B

B sheets: ISO paper sizes slightly larger than A sheets. The ISO standard is used everywhere except North America for determining standard trim sizes.

Bar code: A series of horizontal or vertical parallel lines representing a code that can be optically read and interpreted by a bar code scanner.

Barrel fold: Fold style where the outer edge of each panel or page is folded in toward the other resulting in six panels or pages. Also called *roll fold*.

Baseline: A horizontal line on which type sits.

Basis weight: In the U.S. and Canada, the weight, in pounds, of a ream 500 sheets) of paper cut to basic size.

Bitmap: Computer image composed of pixels.

Blanket: Rubber-coated pad mounted on a cylinder of an offset press that receives the inked image from the plate and transfers it to the paper surface.

Bleed: A printed area that extends beyond the trimmed edge of a printed piece. Bleed areas generally range from ⅛" to ¼" (3.175 mm to 6.35 mm).

Bleeds are produced by printing a piece on a sheet of paper larger than the trim size of the final piece and then cutting away the edges.

Blister pack: Packaging mounted on a card and encased under a plastic dome.

Blueline: A photographic contact print made from plate-ready negatives used as a proof to show positioning of images, cropping, and page sequence. Also called a Dylux or brownline.

Board paper: see *paperboard*

Body copy: see *text*

Boldface: Type that is darker and heavier than the rest of the text with which it is used.

Bond: Grade of paper used for photocopying, envelopes, office correspondence, and flyers.

Brightness: The amount of light reflectivity of a given paper.

Bristol: General term for stock 6 points or thicker with a basis weight between 90# and 200# (200–500 gsm). Used for index cards, file folders, and postcards.

Brownline: see *blueline*

Browser: Software program that allows users to find and decode encrypted documents such as Web pages.

Bulking dummy: A dummy assembled from the paper specified for a printing job.

Butt: To join two elements edge to edge.

C

C sizes: ISO paper sizes with correct dimensions for folders and envelopes for items trimmed to A sizes.

Camera ready: Term describing an image or layout that is ready for print reproduction.

Carbon dioxide: A heavy colorless, odorless gas (associated with global climate change) that results from the combustion of carbon found in organic materials.

Case bind: Binding that uses glue to hold signatures to a case made of binder board covered with paper, plastic, fabric, or leather.

Caption: A word, phrase, or sentence that is placed in close proximity to a photograph, illustration, or other image as a means of clarifying, describing, or identifying it. Also called a *cutline*.

Cast-coated paper: Coated paper with a high-gloss finish achieved by pressing the paper against a metal drum while the clay coating is still wet.

Character: All items on the keyboard, including alphabet letters, numbers, and punctuation.

Chipboard: Solid cardboard used in packaging and for industrial purposes.

Chlorine: A chemical used in the bleaching process to give paper its white appearance and to remove lignin.

Choke: Slightly reducing an image to create a trap.

Cromalin: Color proofing system made from layered colored films exposed from the job's negatives.

CMYK: Stands for cyan, magenta, yellow, and key (black). The primary ink colors that are combined on press or as printed digital output to produce a full range of colors.

Coarse screen: Halftone screen that is less than 100 lpi. Most commonly used for printing on newspaper, fabric, and other rough or highly absorbent surfaces.

Coated paper: Paper with a smooth and sometimes glossy finish created by applying a clay coating to the surface.

Collateral: Ancillary print material used to support an advertising campaign.

Color bars: Strip of colors printed on the edge of four-color process proofs and press sheets to check registration of all colors and to evaluate ink density.

Color break: Where one color stops and another begins.

Color key: Color proofing system made from layered colored films exposed from the job's negatives.

Column: Blocks of type set at the same width.

Comb binding: Binding a publication by inserting the teeth of a flexible plastic comb through holes in a stack of paper.

Condensed type: Type that is narrower than surrounding text.

Continuous-tone image: A photograph or illustration with a range of shades not made up of halftone dots.

Converter: A business that does finishing work on a printed piece, such as making boxes, bags, or envelopes.

Cover stock: Fine printing paper with a basis weight or grammage that is heavier than text or book weight papers.

Creep: Where the middle pages of a folded signature extend slightly beyond the outside pages. Also called *push out* or *thrust*.

Crop: Trimming part of a photograph or illustration so that undesirable or unnecessary elements are eliminated.

Crop marks: Marks placed on the edges of a mechanical to indicate where a printed piece should be trimmed. Also called *trim marks*.

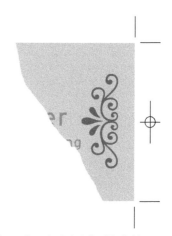

Crop marks are located outside of the final image area and indicate where a piece should be trimmed.

Crossovers: Where a printed area that appears on two-page spread crosses over the gutter. Also called *gutter bleed*.

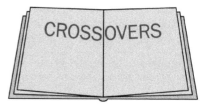

Care must be taken when printing and binding a publication to ensure that crossovers match up on two-page spreads.

Cutline: see *caption*

D

Deboss: To produce a recessed impression on the surface of a paper by pressing it between two dies.

Deckle edge: The edge of paper left ragged as it comes from the papermaking machine.

De-inking: The process of removing ink and other contaminants from collected paper.

Demographics: Statistical data about categories of consumers—e.g., gender, occupation, family size, income, and marital status.

Density: The thickness of a layer of ink.

Descender: The part of a lowercase letter that extends below its baseline as in the letters g, j, p, and y.

Die: Sharp metal rules mounted on a board for making diecuts, or a solid metal block used for stamping foil or an impression on paper.

Diecut: A decorative or unusual cut made in paper with a metal die.

Display type: Type that is larger than text type and used to grab attention. Display type usually conveys a mood or feeling and is not intended to be read in a large body of text.

Direct mail: Form of advertising that uses person-to-person communication by contacting individuals through the postal system.

Dot gain: When halftone dots print larger on paper than they are on films or plates, they reduce detail and lower contrast. Uncoated papers tend to cause more dot gain than coated papers. Also called *dot spread* or *press gain*.

dpi (dots per inch): Used to measure the resolution of a scanned image. Higher dpi produces higher resolution and more detail.

Drawdown: Ink samples specified for a job and applied to the paper specified for the job.

Dry mount: Mounting art or other display materials on a rigid board using heat and pressure rather than wet adhesive.

Dry trapping: Printing an ink or varnish over another layer of ink or varnish after the first layer has dried.

Dull finish: Flat finish on coated paper

Duotone: Halftone made of two colors.

Dylux: see *blueline*

E

Elemental chlorine-free (ECF): A label that indicates fibers have been bleached without elemental chlorine and is instead made with chlorine derivatives such as chlorine dioxide (ClO_2).

Emboss: To produce a raised impression on the surface of paper by pressing it between two dies.

Engraving: Printing method using a metal plate with an image cut into its surface.

EPS (Encapsulated PostScript): Computer file format used for placing images or graphics in documents.

Etched plate: Metal plate that has been etched so that its surface can be used for printing.

Extended typeface: Type that is wider than surrounding text.

F

Fan fold: see *accordion fold*

Felt side: Side of the paper exposed to the felt blanket during the papermaking process. The felt side is considered to be the smoothest side of the paper.

Fifth color: A spot or match color added on press to a four-color print run.

FIM (facing identification mark): A machine-detectable series of vertical bars printed in the upper corner of a business reply card or envelope that allows the U.S. Postal System to automatically cancel letter mail.

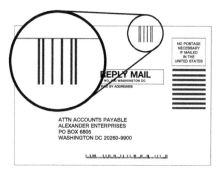

FIMs allow the US Postal Service to automatically cancel business reply cards and letters.

Fine screen: Halftone screen that is 100 lpi or higher. Commonly used for printing on fine printing papers with a smooth, relatively nonabsorbent surface.

Finish: Surface characteristics of paper. Examples of finishes include laid, linen, and vellum.

Flexography: Method of printing on a web press with rubber or soft plastic plates.

Flowlines: (also called thresholds) A horizontal measure that divides a page or an area of space creating alignment points for content.

Flier: Advertising medium that is usually a single 8½" 11" (215.9 279.4 mm) page.

Flood: To print a sheet completely with an ink or varnish.

Flush: A term indicating that type shouldn't be indented but should be set vertically, aligned with the margin.

Foil stamp: Where foil and a heated die is stamped onto paper to form a printed impression.

Folio: The page number and other copy in the lower portion of a page, typically a title or issue date if it's a periodical.

Font: Equipment or software that lets a printing device print a specific typeface of type family.

Forest Stewardship Council (FSC): An independent third-party certifier of sustainably harvested virgin fiber and mixed-use recycled content. www.fsc.org

Form: see *signature*

Four-color process: Method of printing that uses cyan, magenta, yellow, and black to reproduce full-color images. see *CMYK*

FPO: Stands for "For Position Only." FPOs are stand-in replicas of imagery that will be printed. They are typically low-resolution (low-res) versions of high-resolution (high-res) images that are temporarily placed in a digital document to show how an image should be sized and cropped. When the job is printed, the low-res images are replaced with the high-res equivalents.

French fold: Multiple fold where the paper is first folded in half in one direction, then folded in half again, perpendicular to the first fold.

G

Ganging: A cost-saving technique where a number of different items are reproduced at the same time, as in ganging several items on the same sheet of paper or separating several items at the same percentage.

Gathered signatures: Signatures assembled next to each other in the binding process.

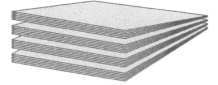

Gathered signatures are bound side by side.

Gatefold: A folding style where the outer edges fold inward to meet in the gutter, and then folded again at the point where they meet to form eight panels or pages.

GIF or .gif (Graphics Interchange Format): An 8-bit, low-memory option for posting images online.

Grade: A term used to distinguish between various qualities of printing papers. Examples of grades include premium and grades 1 through 5 for coated papers.

Grammage: The European and Asian method of measuring paper weight by representing the gram weight of one square meter of paper, expressed as grams per square meter or gsm.

Graphic arts: The trades, industries, and professions related to designing and printing on paper and other substrates.

Gravure: Printing process where the matter to be printed is etched into the printing surface. Also called *intaglio*.

Grayscale image: A continuous-tone black-and-white image such as a photograph or illustration.

Grid: The invisible framework on which a page is designed.

Gripper edge: The leading edge of a sheet of paper clamped by metal grippers as it is pulled through the printing press, typically about 3/8" (9.525 mm). Also called the *gripper margin*.

Grippers: The press mechanism that draws the paper through the cylinders of the press.

Gutter: The white space between columns of type or between pages on a two-page spread.

Gutter bleed: see *crossover*

H

Hairline: Minute amount of space used to describe a thin rule or close register.

Halftone: Reproducing a continuous tone image by photographing it through a fine screen to convert the image into a series of dots.

Halftone dot: Units in a halftone that, by their various sizes, re-create a continuous tone image.

A halftone screen allows a continuous tone image to print by converting it into a series of dots.

Haze: see *scum*

Headline: A sentence, phrase, word, or group of words set in large, bold type above the text on a page.

Hickey: A spot or imperfection on a printed piece that occurs during the print run because of a speck of dust or other particle on the press interfered with the ink's application on paper.

High-res: A digital image with a resolution of 200 dpi or more.

Holdout: see *ink holdout*

Holography: Producing the appearance of a three-dimensional image by using a laser to overlay embossed images onto film and then onto paper.

Hue: A specific color.

I

Image: Visual counterpart or likeness of an object, person, or a scene produced as an illustration or photograph.

Imagesetter: A device for outputting proofs and similar printed images or printing plates but not intended for printing multiple copies.

Imposition: An arrangement of pages on a printed sheet that enables them to be in the correct order when the sheet is folded and trimmed.

Impressions per hour (iph): A means of measuring the speed of a press.

Imprint: To print new copy on a previously printed sheet.

Indicia: Recognized by the U.S. postal system as a means of showing that postage has been paid. Mailers using an indicia must have a bulk mailing permit.

```
BULK RATE
U.S. POSTAGE
PAID
CINCINNATI, OH
PERMIT NO. 0000
```

```
NONPROFIT ORG.
U.S. POSTAGE
PAID
SAN JUAN, PR
PERMIT NO. 0000
```

Indicias are printed on an envelope where a stamp would normally go to show that postage has been paid. A properly designed indicia identifies the user, their permit number, and the classification or rate code of the mailing.

Industrial papers: Papers produced for uses other than printing. Examples include kraft paper and chipboard.

Ink fountain: Printing press mechanism that stores and supplies ink to the printing plate or other image carrier. Rollers then transfer the ink from the fountain to the plate.

Ink holdout: Characteristic of a paper that prevents it from absorbing ink, allowing ink to dry on the paper's surface. Also called *holdout*.

Inline: Any operation tied to the printing process and done on press such as varnishing or folding.

Intact Forests: see *old growth*

Internet: A network of linked computers and networks that use the same set of communications protocols.

Intaglio: see *gravure*

ISO standards: Metric measurement system for paper sizes in Europe and Asia.

Italic: Type style with characters slanted to the right. Used to emphasize a word or passage.

J

Jogging: To straighten or align the edges of a stack of paper by jostling them.

JPEG: File format designated by the Joint Photographic Experts Group for image compression. JPEGs are frequently used for placing imagery in websites and online applications.

K

Kerning: Adjusting the amount of space between letters or characters so that letter spacing appears to be in balance. *See letterspacing*

PLAY

Before kerning

PLAY

After kerning. The space has been adjusted between the letterforms so that spacing appears more balanced.

Kiss die cut: A process used for peel-off labels where a die cut is made through the face materials but not the backing.

Kraft: Strong paper made from unbleached wood pulp that is often used for paper bags and wrapping paper.

L

Laminate: A means of bonding plastic film to a sheet of paper using heat and pressure.

Leading: The amount of vertical space between lines of type.

Lenticular printing: Printing process involving animated effects that flip back and forth as the viewing angle changes.

Letterpress: The process of printing from an inked raised surface.

Letterspacing: Modifying the distance between the letters in a word. Also called *tracking* or *kerning*.

Before letterspacing

After letterspacing

Line art: A black-and-white image that is not continuous tone or does not include any grays. Also called *line drawing* or *line copy*.

Line count: see *screen ruling*

Lithography: The process of printing from a flat surface (such as a smooth stone or metal plate) that has been treated so that the image area is ink receptive and the nonimage area is ink repellant.

Logo: A unique design, symbol, or typographic treatment that represents a company or brand.

Logotype: A logo comprising typographic forms, usually a unique typographic treatment of a company's name.

Low-res: A digital image with a resolution of 100 dpi or less.

lpi (lines per inch): A means of measuring the fineness of a halftone screen by measuring the number of dots per inch in a halftone screen.

M

Makeready: Getting a printing press ready for a print run by filling the ink fountains, adjusting the paper feeder, etc.

Margin: White space at the top, bottom, and to the left and right of a body of type.

Masthead: The name of a newspaper, magazine, or other periodical displayed on the cover. Also used to describe the area where a periodical and its publisher's name, address, and staff credits appear.

Match color: Flat ink colors that are matched to swatches. Also called *spot color.*

Matchprint: A digital proof that uses toner to replicate the process colors. Matchprints are *close* to cromalin color accuracy but are markedly less expensive.

Mask: A means of isolating a portion of an image from its surrounding area so that it becomes a silhouette or outline image.

Matte: A flat, not glossy, finish on a paper or photograph.

Mechanical: A document with type, graphic elements, and imagery in position.

Moiré: Undesirable patterns in printed halftones caused by improperly aligned screens.

A Moiré often occurs when a printed halftone is screened again as it is made into a halftone.

Mottle: Spotty, uneven ink absorption resulting in blotchy image reproduction.

Multicolor printing: Printing with more than one color but fewer than four colors.

N

Native file format: A file saved in the application in which it was created. Native file formats can't be transferred from one application to the next.

Nested signature: Where signatures are assembled inside one another before binding.

This drawing illustrates the assembly of three nested signatures prior to binding.

Newsletter: Information sheet or several sheets usually styled like a small newspaper.

O

Observational research: A research technique where the subjects are observed in their natural settings either with or without their knowledge

Offset lithography: Mostly commonly used method of printing where an image on a plate is offset onto a rubber blanket cylinder which, in turn, transfers the image to a sheet of paper.

Old growth: Also called intact forests are natural forests that have been allowed to grow naturally over a long period of time (in excess of 100 years).

Opacity: Characteristic of paper that prevents printing on one side from showing through on the other.

Optical Character Recognition (OCR): Automatic computer input process where a scanner reads printed characters and symbols and converts them to electronic data.

Outline image: see *silhouette image*

Overrun: Excess production to compensate for spoilage, future requests for materials, and other unanticipated needs.

P

Paperboard: Index stock over 110# and cover stock over 80# or 200 gsm commonly used in packaging. Also called *board paper*.

PDF (Portable Document Format): Digital file format that allows documents to be viewed and printed independent of the application used to create them.

Perfect binding: A method of binding magazines, books, and other publications in which the signatures are glued to the cover and held together with a strip of adhesive.

Pica: Unit of typographic measure equal to 0.166 inch (4.218 mm).

PICT: Macintosh image file format.

Preconsumer waste: Refers to materials that include trip or scrap from the manufacturing process and printers, or even overruns that are reused to make new products.

Prepress: Preparing a job for print reproduction by performing necessary functions such as separating, color correcting, and impositioning the pages.

PMS: Stands for Pantone Matching System, a means of specifying match or spot colors and their ink formulations.

Point: A typographic measurement system used for measuring the height of type, thickness of rules, and leading.

Postconsumer waste: End product that has reached the consumer used and then collected to make new material rather than end up in a landfill or incinerator. This is what is referred to when most people think of recycled paper.

PostScript: Computer language that allows digital files to be printed on desktop printers and imagesetters.

Press gain: see *dot gain*

Pressure-sensitive label: A label with an adhesive backing that can be peeled off, and the label applied to another surface by pressure.

Printer font: A font that allows a printing device to output a typeface.

Printer's spreads: Pages that are set up so they are impositioned exactly where they will be when a publication is folded and printed.

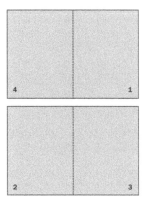

When a four-page signature is set up as printer's spreads, pages 2 and 3, and pages 1 and 4 face each other.

Printing plate: A surface carrying an image to be printed.

Processed chlorine-free (PCF): A label used to refer to recycled fiber that was not bleached using chlorine or chlorine derivatives but that may have been bleached using chlorine during the paper's initial production and therefore may not be totally chlorine free.

Process color: The inks used in four-color process printing. Ink colors consist of cyan, magenta, yellow, and black.

Proof: A test sheet made to represent how a final printed product will look so that flaws may be corrected before the piece is printed.

Psychographics: A technique that seeks to identify motivating factors for various groups of people. Often based on demographic data.

Q

Quadratone: Halftone comprising four colors, usually to create a rich tonal range but not comprising the four process colors (cyan, yellow, magenta, and black).

R

Raster image processing (RIP): Converting digital files to bitmapped images that can be output on an imagesetter. The rocess is described as "ripping a file."

Reader's spreads: Pages that are set up as they will be read (left- and right-hand pages side by side.)

Ream: Five hundred sheets of paper.

Recycled paper: Paper coming from either post- or preconsumer waste. Recycled pulp can be made into the same variety and quality of paper stock that is made from virgin fiber.

Reflective art: Photographs, illustrations, and other imagery that is scanned or viewed as an item that reflects light. Also called *reflective copy, hard copy, or reflective imagery.*

Register: When each sheet enters the press from precisely the same position ensuring that all colors are in "register."

Register marks: Targetlike symbol placed in exactly the same spot for each color plate so that proper alignment of the colors will occur on press.

Register marks help printers keep colors in alignment as a piece passes through the different ink stations on a press.

Resolution: The quantification of print quality using the number of dots per inch in electronic imaging.

Reverse: A white or noncolor image against a dark, inked, or colored background.

RGB: Stands for red, green, and blue, additive primary colors that are used to create a full range of color as projected light on a computer screen.

Roll fold: see *barrel fold*

Rule: A line set as part of typesetting.

S

Saddle stitch: A method of binding by stitching through the centerfold of nested signatures.

Saturation: The degree to which a color is pure and free of dilution from black, white, or gray.

Scanner: A device that converts images on film or paper into digital information.

Score: To crease or indent paper along a straight line so it folds more easily and accurately.

Screen font: Font that can be viewed on a computer monitor.

Screen printing: see *silk screen*

Screen ruling: Number of rows or lines of dots per inch in a screen for making a screen tint or halftone. Also called *line count*, *screen frequency*, *screen size*, or *screen value*.

Screw and post binding: Binding that secures pages with a bolt that is inserted through a drilled hole and secured with a post on the opposite side.

Scum: A thin haze of ink that appears in on-image areas on a printed sheet. Also called *haze*.

Separations: Reproducing a color image by dividing it into four negatives, one each for cyan, magenta, yellow, and black.

Serigraphy: see *silk screen*

Server: A computer connected to the Internet that allows pages or sites that you have placed on it to be called up or displayed by users browsers.

Sheetfed: A printing process utilizing sheets of paper rather than rolls.

Shingling: The allowance made during page impositioning to compensate for creep. Also called *stair stepping* or *progressive margins*.

Show through: Areas where an image printed on one side of a sheet can be seen on the opposite side. Show through occurs when the paper is too thin for the ink application.

Shrink-wrap: A method of securely wrapping packages, loose items, or products in clear plastic film.

Side stitch: To bind by stapling through pages along one edge. Also called *side wire*.

Signature: A printed sheet folded at least once, possibly many times, to become part of a book, magazine, or other publication. Signatures are commonly made up of four, eight, sixteen, or thirty-two pages. Also called a *form*.

Silk screen: A method of printing where ink is forced through a stencil adhered to a screen. Also called *serigraphy* or *screen printing*.

Silhouette halftone: A halftone image from which the background has been removed, usually through masking. Also called *outline halftone*.

Small caps: Capital letters smaller than the capital letters in a typeface.

Spoilage: Paper that is recycled as a result of on-press mistakes and accidents.

Spot color: see *match color*

Spread: Slightly enlarging an image to create a trap.

Stet: Latin for "let it stand." Proofreader's or editor's indication that an item marked for correction should remain as it was before the correction.

Supercalendered: Paper that has passed through metal and fiber rollers to produce a smooth, glossy finish.

SWOP (Specifications for Web Offset Publications): Recommended printing specifications published every few years by a committee of graphic arts professionals.

Symmetry: The correspondence in form so that parts on opposite sides of a page, line, or plane appear alike.

T

Text: The body of written material on a page or document. Also called *body copy*.

Text paper: Fine printing papers with a basis weight or grammage that falls in-between cover and writing or bond weights.

Thermography: A method of printing where a raised impression is created by heat curing a blend of ink and resin.

TIFF (Tagged Image File Format): Used for placing images or graphics in documents created in word processing, page layout, or drawing programs.

Tint: see *value*

Tonal range: Difference between the darkest and lightest area of a continuous tone image.

Tonal compression: The reduction of the tonal range in an image to facilitate image reproduction.

Totally chlorine-free (TCF): A label that indicates fiber has been produced without the use of chlorine in the bleaching process or is unbleached.

Tracking: see *letterspacing*

Trademark: A slogan, name, or identifying symbol used to represent a company, product or brand.

Transparency: Photographic reproduction such as a 35mm slide that is produced with a camera on transparent film.

Transparent ink: Ink that allows for blending through overlapping colors. Example: four-color process inks.

Trap: Printing one ink over another so there is a slight overlap of colors in order to prevent a colorless gap between adjacent colors if they are slightly off register.

Tray: A relatively shallow folding carton with a bottom hinged to the wide side and end walls.

Tree-free: Includes paper products made from agricultural residues, nontree fibers and more recently products made from minerals and plastics.

Trim marks: see *crop marks*

Tritone: A halftone made from three colors.

Tube: A carton in the shape of a rectangular sleeve formed from a sheet of board that is folded over and glued against its edges.

Typeface: Design of alphabetic letters, numerals, and symbols unified by consistent visual properties. Typeface designs are identified by name, such as Helvetica or Garamond.

Type family: A range of style variations based on a single typeface design.

Type style: Modifications in a typeface that create design variety while maintaining the visual character of the typeface. These include variations in weight (light, medium or bold), width (condensed or extended), or angle (italic or slanted versus roman or upright).

U

Uncoated paper: Paper that has not been coated with clay.

Unit cost: The cost of one item in a print run arrived at by dividing the total cost of production by the number of pieces produced.

Unsharp masking: Adjusting an image digitally to make it appear as though it is in better focus.

UV or ultraviolet coating: Liquid applied to a sheet of paper that his heat cured with ultraviolet light, resulting in a hard, durable finish.

V

Value: The lightness or darkness of a color. Darker values where black is added are called *shades*. Lighter values where white is added are called *tints* or *pastels*.

Varnish: Coating applied to paper to give it a dull or glossy finish or to provide protection against scuffing and fingerprints.

Vector: Graphics that are made up using mathematical equations based on straight lines and curves. Vector graphics are infinitely scaleable.

Volatile organic compounds (VOCs): Refers to a broad class of organic gasses that includes vapors from solvents, inks, and gasoline and can react with other materials to form ozone, the major ingredient of smog.

Virgin fiber: Refers to paper pulp fiber that is derived directly from its organic source.

W

Watermark: A translucent impression made in a sheet of paper created during its manufacture.

Web-fed: A printing process utilizing paper fed through the press from a roll.

Wet trapping: Printing an ink or varnish over another layer of ink or varnish while the bottom layer is still wet.

Widow: A word or part of a word that is the last line of a paragraph or that ends up at the top of a page by itself.

Wire-O binding: A binding method that winds a circular, double-wire strip through prepunched holes in the cover and pages of a publication.

Wire side: In the papermaking process, the side of the paper that is formed against the wire. The wire side of paper made on a fourdrinier machine is generally rougher. For paper made on a cylinder machine, the wire side is generally smoother.

Window envelope: An envelope with an opening where part of the contents can be seen.

Work and tumble: Printing a sheet so that the same image is produced on both sides of a sheet. When the sheet is tumbled, the opposite side of the sheet is fed through the press.

Work and turn: Printing a sheet so that the same image is produced on both sides of a sheet. When the sheet is turned, the same side of the sheet is fed through the press.

Writing paper: Lightweight paper used for correspondence.

Wrong reading: An image that is backwards when compared to the original.

Resources and Recommended Reading

PROFESSIONAL ORGANIZATIONS

American Institute of Graphic Arts,
www.aiga.org
The largest membership-based graphic design organization. Since 1914, the AIGA has been a place for creative professionals to network and work towards improving graphic design as a profession.

International Council of Graphic Design Associations, www.icograda.org
Founded in 1963 to establish best practices for the design community.

Art Directors Club, www.adcglobal.org
Founded in 1920 to clarify the relationship between advertising art and fine art and exists today to inspire creativity in the design industry.

Type Directors Club, www.tdc.org
Founded in 1946 to support the best of type design.

Society of Publication Designers,
www.spd.org
Founded 1965 to support trade, corporate, institutional, newspaper and editorial design.

Society of News Design, www.snd.org
Founded in 1964 to enhance communication around the world through excellence in visual journalism.

Society of Illustrators,
www.societyillustrators.org
Founded in 1901 to promote the art of illustration.

One Club, www.oneclub.org
Founded in 1961 to promote excellence in advertising.

IxDA, www.ixda.org
Founded in 2003 to advance the discipline of Interaction Design.

Usability Professionals Association,
www.upassoc.org
Founded in 1991 for usability professionals to promote usability concepts and techniques worldwide.

Graphic Artists Guild, www.gag.org
Founded 1967, Detroit, USA. For American visual creatives (design, web, illustration). A union of professionals who have come together to pursue common goals, share their experience, raise industry standards, and improve their ability to achieve satisfying and rewarding careers. Producers of the book "Handbook of Pricing and Ethical Guidelines".

Color Association of the United States,
www.colorassociation.com
Founded 1915, NY, USA. For all designers who use color. Color forecasting organization holding extensive color archives, trend information, custom color consulting and publications.

Society for Environmental Graphic Design,
www.segd.org
Global community of people who work at
the intersection of communication design
and the built environment. Embraces
many design disciplines including graphic,
architectural, interior, landscape, and
industrial design, all concerned with the
visual aspects of wayfinding, communicating identity and information, and shaping
the idea of place.

TYPE FOUNDRIES

Hoefler & Frere-Jones (H&FJ),
typography.com

Emigre, emegre.com

Vllg, vllg.com

MyFonts, myfonts.com

PACKAGING DESIGN AND PRODUCTION

Design Matters: Packaging 01 An Essential
Primer for Today's Competitive Market
Capsule
Rockport Publishers, 2008

Design Secrets: Packaging
Fishel, Catharine
Rockport Publishers, 2003

Design and Technology of Packaging
Decoration for the Consumer Market
Giles, Geoff A., ed
CRC Press, 2000

Package Design Workbook: The Art and
Science of Successful Packaging
Braue-DuPuis
Rockport Publishers, 2008

Packaging Design
Stewart, Bill Laurence
King Publishers, 2007

What Is Packaging Design?
Calver, Giles
RotoVision 2007

RF Measurements of Die and Packaging
Wartenburg, Scott A.
Artech House, 2002

The Packaging and Design Templates
Sourcebook 2
Herriott, Luke
RotoVision, 2010

Packaging Templates
Hai, Ju
Gingko Press, 2009

The Production Manual
Ambrose, Gavin; Harris, Paul
AVA Publishing SA, 2008

PROOFREADING AND COPYWRITING

The Associated Press Style Book and Libel
Manual Associated Press
Addison-Wesley Publishing Company,
1982

Chicago Manual of Style, 16th Edition
University of Chicago Press 2010
www.chicagomanualofstyle.org

Grammatically Correct: The Writer's Essential Guide to Punctuation, Spelling, Style, Usage and Grammar Stillman, Anne
Writers Digest Books, 1997

The Associated Press Guide to Punctuation
Cappon, Renee J. and Jack, ed
Perseus Publishing, 2003

The Elements of Style
Strunk, William, Jr.; and White, E. B.
Pearson Allyn & Bacon, 2000

The Elements of Technical Writing
Blake, Gary; and Bly, Robert
Pearson Higher Education, 2000

The Little, Brown Handbook, Fifth Edition
Fowler, Ramsey H.; Aaron, Jane E.
HarperCollins Publishers Inc., 1992

Acronym Finder www.acronymfinder.com

Dictionary.com www.dictionary.com

Grammar Now! www.grammarnow.com

SUSTAINABLE DESIGN AND PRODUCTION

SustainAble: A handbook of materials and applications for graphic designers and their clients Sherin, Aaris Rockport
Publishers, 2008

AIGA Center for Sustainable Design
www.sustainability.aiga.org

ConserveaTree
www.conservatree.com

Design by Nature
www.designbynature.org

Environmental Paper Network
www.environmentalpaper.org

GreenBlue
www.greenblue.org,
www.sustainablepackaging.org

Institute for Sustainable Communications (ISC)
www.sustaincom.org

MetaFore
www.metafore.org

O2 Global Network
www.o2.org
Re-nourish
www.re-nourish.com

Waterless Printing Association (WPA)
www.waterless.org

UX/UI DESIGN

Communicating Design: Developing Web Site Documentation for Design and Planning
Brown, Dan M.
New Riders Press, 2006

Don't Make Me Think: A Commonsense Approach to Web Usability, Second Edition
Krug, Steve
New Riders Press, 2005

Sketching User Experience
Buxton, Bill
Elsevier, 2007

Smashing UX Design
Allen, Jesmond; Chudley, James John
Wiley & Sons, Ltd, 2012

The Handbook of Global User Research
Schumacher, Robert M.
Elsevier, 2010

Designing Interactions
Moggridge, Bill
MIT Press, 2007

GRID AND LAYOUT DESIGN

Grid Systems Elam,
Kimberly Princeton
Architectural Press, 2004

Making and Breaking the Grid: A Graphic
Design Layout Workshop
Samara, Timothy
Rockport Publishers, 2002

Layout Workbook: A Real-World Guide to
Building Pages in Graphic Design
Cullen, Kristin Rockport Publishers, 2005

IMAGING AND COLOR

A Guide to Graphic Print Production
Johansso, Kaj; Lundberg, Peter; and
Ryberg, Robert John Wiley & Sons, 2003

Color Design Workbook: A Real-World
Guide to Using Color in Graphic Design
AdamsMorioka with Stone, Terry Rockport
Publishers, 2006

Color Index: Over 1100 Color
Combinations, CMYK and RGB Formulas,
for Print and Web Media
Krause, Jim
How Design Books, 2002

Pocket Pal
International Paper Staff
International Paper, 1998

Print Production Essentials
O'Connor, Kevin
Macmillan Publishing Company, 2003

Real World Color Management
Fraser, Bruce
Peachpit Press, 2003

The Complete Color Harmony
Sutton, Tina; and Whelan, Bride M.
Rockport Publishers, 2004

The Designer's Guide to Color
Combinations
Carbaga, Leslie
North Light Books, 2003

TYPOGRAPHY

Adobe Type Library Reference Book
Adobe Systems
Adobe Press, 2007

Designing Typefaces
Earls, David
RotoVision, 2003

Designing with Type: A Basic Course in
Typography
Craig, James; Bevington, William; and
Meyer, Susan E., ed.
Watson-Guptill Publications, 1999

Typography Workbook: A Real-World Guide
to Using Type in Graphic Design
Samara, Timothy
Rockport Publishers, 2006

Stop Stealing Sheep and Find Out How
Type Works
Spiekermann, Eric; and Ginger, E. M.
Adobe Press, 2002

The Complete Manual of Typography
Felici, James
Adobe Press, 2002

The Elements of Typographic Style
Bringhurst, Robert
Harley & Marks Publishers, 1992

*Type, Image, Message: A Graphic Design
Layout Workshop*
Skolos, Nancy; and Wedell, Thomas
Rockport Publishers, 2006

*Thinking with Type, 2nd revised and
expanded edition: A Critical Guide for
Designers, Writers, Editors, & Students*
Lupton, Ellen
Princeton Architectural Press, 2004, 2010

The Fundamentals of Typography
Ambrose, Gavin; Harris, Paul
AVA Publishing, 2006

*Type rules, Third Edition: the designer's
guide to professional typography*
Strizver, Ilene
John Wiley & Sons, 2010

DOMAIN REGISTRAR COMPANIES

www.godaddy.com
www.networksolutions.com
www.mydomain.com
www.register.com

WEB HOSTING COMPANIES

www.inmotionhosting.com
www.webhostinghub.com
www.arvixe.com

GENERAL DESIGN

*Graphic Designer's Guide to Pricing,
Estimating & Budgeting*
Williams, Theo Stephan
Allworth Press, 2001

*Idea Index: Graphic Effects and
Typographic Treatments*
Krause, Jim
North Light Books, 2003

*Universal Principles of Design: 100 Ways
to Enhance Usability, Influence Perception,
Increase Appeal, Make Better Design
Decisions, and Teach through Design*
Lidwell, William; Holden, Kritina; and
Butler, Jill
Rockport Publishers, 2003

Design Elements, A Graphic Style Manual
Samara, Timothy
Rockport Publishers, 2007

*Design Matters: Logos 01
An Essential Primer for Today's
Competitive Market*
Capsule
Rockport Publishers, 2007

*Design Matters: Brochures 01
An Essential Primer for Today's
Competitive Market*
Taute, Michelle
Rockport Publishers, 2007

Design Matters: Packaging 01
An Essential Primer for Today's Market

Graphic Design The New Basics
Lupton, Ellen; Phillips, Jennifer Cole
Princeton Architectural Press, 2008

Index

About the Authors

Poppy Evans is an award-winning writer and graphic designer. She has written more than 200 articles, which have appeared in *Print*, *HOW*, *Step Inside Design*, and other design trade magazines. She is also the author of thirteen books, including *The Designer's Survival Handbook*, *Exploring the Elements of Design*, and *Extraordinary Graphics for Unusual Surfaces*. She is assistant professor of communication arts at the Art Academy of Cincinnati and lives in Park Hills, Kentucky.

Aaris Sherin is an educator, writer, and designer. She is currently an assistant professor of graphic design at St. John's University in Queens, New York. With research interests spanning both historical and contemporary issues, Sherin works in areas that include sustainable design practice and theory, the history of women in design, and hybrid research practices. Sherin uses original source material and journalistic methods to uncover areas of design practice that have been overlooked and/or merit greater attention. She is the author of *SustainAble: A handbook of materials and applications for graphic designers and their clients*, (Rockport Publishers, 2008). As guest editor for *GroveArt* (Oxford University Press), Sherin supervised the addition of more than thirty entries on female designers
as part of the 2006 Women in the Arts update. Sherin is a frequent lecturer and speaker at both national and international design conferences. Her writing has been featured in *PRINT Magazine*, *STEP Inside Design*, *GroveArt* (Oxford University Press), and *Leonardo* (MIT Press).

ACKNOWLEDGMENTS

Thanks to the following individuals whose expertise helped greatly in compiling information for this book:

Michaelle Keyes, Landor Associates
Ellen Weaver, Digitas LLC
Valerie Lucio, USPS
Kim McKnight, Cincinnati Graphic Coatings

CPSIA information can be obtained
at www.ICGtesting.com
Printed in the USA
LVHW071136140319
610241LV00015B/8/P